Your Towns and Cities in the Great War

Isle of Wight
in the Great War

Your Towns and Cities in the Great War

Isle of Wight
in the Great War

M.J. Trow

Pen & Sword
MILITARY

First published in Great Britain in 2015 by
PEN & SWORD MILITARY
an imprint of
Pen and Sword Books Ltd
47 Church Street
Barnsley
South Yorkshire S70 2AS

ISBN 9781783463015

Printed and bound in England
by CPI Group (UK) Ltd, Croydon, CR0 4YY

Typeset in Times New Roman

Pen & Sword Books Ltd incorporates the imprints of
Pen & Sword Archaeology, Atlas, Aviation, Battleground, Discovery,
Family History, History, Maritime, Military, Naval, Politics, Railways,
Select, Social History, Transport, True Crime, and Claymore Press,
Frontline Books, Leo Cooper, Praetorian Press, Remember When,
Seaforth Publishing and Wharncliffe.
For a complete list of Pen and Sword titles please contact
Pen and Sword Books Limited
47 Church Street, Barnsley, South Yorkshire, S70 2AS, England
E-mail: enquiries@pen-and-sword.co.uk
Website: **www.pen-and-sword.co.uk**

Contents

Acknowledgements

Thank you to all the Islanders who have contributed memories or images for this book, but in particular, I would like to thank: Elizabeth Boxall, John Brett, Jean Downer, Beryl Flux, Andrew Greenham, Rosemary Matthews, Steve Munns, Gary Ranson, Raymond Saunders, Brian Shipman, Richard Smout and his team at the Isle of Wight Record Office, Mrs L Trickett, David Yates and the *Isle of Wight County Press*. All images remain the copyright of the owner.

As always, my thanks also go to my wife Carol, indefatigable researcher, typist and all-round support in everything I do.

And a final thank you to those of the Isle of Wight who gave their lives in the Great War for Civilization, 1914-18.

Chapter One

1914: For King and Country

ON THE AFTERNOON of Sunday, 28 June 1914, a car took a wrong turning in Sarajevo, a small and unimportant Bosnian town. In the back seat rode the Archduke Franz Ferdinand, heir to the throne of Austria and his wife Sophie. The open-topped limousine purred past a pavement café where a 19-year-old student, Gavrilo Princip, sat in astonishment. He was astonished because he believed Franz Ferdinand and Sophie were dead already, the victims of an assassin's bomb, thrown earlier in the day. He pulled himself together, walked up to the almost stationary car and pulled the trigger of his revolver twice. Sophie died almost instantly; Franz Ferdinand minutes later. Their deaths sparked the Great War and four years later, an estimated 16 million men were dead with a further 20 million wounded.

The summer of 1914 was a scorcher, 1300 miles away from Sarajevo in the Isle of Wight. Ladies in white frothy dresses and parasols wandered the sea fronts of Ventnor, Sandown, Shanklin and Ryde on the arms of men with boaters and striped blazers. There was ice cream and candy floss (called cotton candy, then), penny slot machines along the Island's many piers and pretty children

Archduke Franz Ferdinand his wife Sophia and their three children Prince Ernest, Prince Maximilian and Princess Sophia.

Archduke Franz Ferdinand and his wife lying in State at the Burgkapelle, Vienna.

laughed and played at the water's edge where the bathing machines stood. The Island's hotels were full and scores of German waiters bustled about in white aprons serving the guests and the day-trippers. The German waiter was something of a caricature at the time and there are examples later, in France, when 'Tommies' from the British trenches would call 'Waiter!' to their opposite numbers across No Man's Land. Island bookshops sold the brand new book by Miss Wylie, published by Mills and Boon and called *Eight Years in Germany*. 'The German is the world's pagan,' Miss Wylie wrote and tried to correct the rather dim view that most Britons had of them.

The Isle of Wight was no stranger to Germans. For years after the death of Victoria in 1901, her nephew, the Kaiser, Wilhelm II, stayed at Osborne and raced his yacht during Cowes Week. Various writers in the local and national press, once the war was underway, laid the blame for it squarely on the German emperor's shoulders – 'It is now quite evident,' said the editor of the Island's *County Press* in October,

> 'that when, only a few years ago, the Kaiser visited England, he was plotting against us while professing friendship for us. Sweet words were on his lips, but in his heart was bitter hate ...'

Edward VII had summed up his nephew better years before when he said, 'It is not by his will that he will unleash a war, but by his weakness.'

Edwin (Ted) Kingswell survived the war. He was a stoker on HMS *Canopus*, launched at Portsmouth in 1897. The ship took part in the hunt for Admiral Graf Spee's Asia squadron early in the war and was involved in the naval bombardment of Gallipoli from the Dardanelles.
(Yates)

Pre-Dreadnought battleship HMS *Canopus* armed with four 12-inch and twelve 6-inch guns; with a speed of 18 knots.

The local newspapers carried no hint of trouble during July although that was a month of frantic diplomacy as the major powers in Europe called in favours and put their military might behind the paper promises of various treaties signed since the 1880s. All holiday-makers had to do to reassure themselves that all was well was to look out into the sea-roads of the Solent where the annual Fleet Review took place on 18 July. Flags of all colours fluttered from the halyards of the Dreadnoughts, the most powerful warships in the world. The German *Kreigsmarine* might boast twenty ships of this class, but we had thirty; all would be well in the (unlikely) event of conflict. And to prove that the 20th century had dawned, there were four airships, eight aeroplanes and twenty seaplanes. This was the largest navy in the world, with more ships than any other two of the world's nations put together.

Revisionist historians today put responsibility for the First World War squarely on the over-ambitious militarism of the new Germany (which was largely the British view in 1914), but it was far more complicated than that and everyone involved, the Central Powers and the Allies, believed that the war would be fluid and swift; certainly it would be all over by Christmas. Britain declared war on 4 August, only because the Germans had invaded Belgium and treaty obligations stretching back to 1839 gave us no choice. The *Isle of Wight*

German infantry advancing into Belgium in August 1914. Thirty miles a day had to be achieved by soldiers of the First Army to conform to the Schlieffen Plan.

Observer spoke for the entire nation – 'the warlike bureaucracies of Berlin and Vienna' had decided on the 'arbitrament of the sword'.

'There are things which are more precious even than peace and one of these is honour ... We go into this war with clean hands and the highest of motives ... and, terrible as we know it must be, we enter upon it with calmness and confidence.'

The Island braced itself. Four miles across the Solent from Ryde is Portsmouth, the home of the Royal Navy. The Germans had been involved in a naval arms race with us for ten years and had been building an unknown number of submarines – *Untersee* boats, which would become a terrifying new weapon of the war. It is odd that, in an Island like the Wight, part of the outer defences of Portsmouth, relatively little is made of the Navy. Comments in the local Press are few and of the correspondents who provided me with family information for this book, there is no paperwork and only one photograph of a sailor.

This is largely because the Navy was usually far away, blockading Germany or defending the far-flung Empire and much of what they did was routine. Their work was essential to the war effort, especially in keeping the Merchant fleet going and Britain fed, but it was unspectacular. The only major battle at sea was fought at Jutland in 1916 (see Chapter 3) and unlike the *Kreigsmarine* which was hugely proud of its U-boats, submarines in the Royal Navy were regarded by British civilians as rather 'sneaky'.

The local Red Cross formed a Men's Detachment and practised their first aid at every opportunity. No one knew exactly what the war would bring, but at the back of everyone's mind (and still being warned against as late as 1917) was the risk of invasion. Everybody had to be ready. Firework displays and concerts were cancelled early in August; the season came to an abrupt halt. There were worries over unemployment as a result of the blow that was bound to fall on the tourist industry. The superstitious worried about an impending eclipse of the sun – what could it mean for the war now underway?

Under a new section called *War Items*, local newspapers like the *Observer* and the *County Press* told the public that no volunteer serviceman would lose his right to vote and Post Offices took on the task of sticking accurate war news up in their windows. The accuracy of this news must be called into question. At first, Lord Kitchener, the Secretary of State for War, refused to allow journalists anywhere near the Front for fear of betraying secrets to the enemy via the British Press. This meant that first reports were vague and hopelessly out of date, especially in provincial papers which relied on the National Press as their source of information. A Press Bureau was set up by Winston Churchill, First Lord of the Admiralty, but it could only print expurgated news so that Fleet Street called it the 'Suppress Bureau'. Even weather reports from France were censored and Lord Rothermere, the newspaper magnate, admitted later, 'We're telling lies; we know we're telling lies; we daren't tell the truth.'

Cowes and East Cowes were the only Island towns engaged in heavy industry and the shipbuilders J S White were already building destroyers. These had been ordered by the Chilean government but there was talk of a greater need for them here instead. Sir Charles Seeley, one of the Island's largest landowners, turned over his imposing house at Brooke for Red Cross use and the Royal Garrison Artillery stationed at various forts on the Island were put through their paces. The huge fort on Culver Down was fitted with anti-aircraft guns.

War in the air was an unknown in 1914 and very few Islanders had ever seen a plane, except those who had gone along, fascinated, to see the wreckage of one that had come down on the Island four years earlier. Its pilot, who escaped unharmed, was Captain Robert Loraine later commissioned in the Royal Flying Corps, an actor who flew under the pseudonym of Jones. He would win the Military Cross during the war for bringing down a German Albatross over the Western Front and is credited with the invention of the word 'joystick'. Attacks on civilians from the air were the stuff of nightmare, of the warped imagination of writers like H G Wells. But reality had caught up with fiction by 1914. The Solent was closed to all unauthorized traffic and the guns of the Needles Battery

The main gate to Culver Down Fort overlooking the Eastern Approaches to the Solent. Anti-aircraft guns were installed here during the First World War. *(Trow)*

fired over the bows of two tramp steamers sailing there against orders.

All forts and other installations were no-go areas, with barbed wire springing up in all directions. The Island's fortifications network and the barracks with their compounds were Victorian buildings of imposing red brick. Ostensibly defended by the Royal Garrison Artillery, all sorts of units were housed in them temporarily during the war on their way to the Front. Some of them slept in railway carriages. Most of the forts, like Golden Hill, had their own hospitals. The army and navy collaborated in the opening months of the war, altering the gun ports to accommodate the new technology, for example of anti-aircraft weapons. 'Palmerston's Follies', built in the Solent to guard against a possible French invasion in 1859-60, underwent changes too. Signs warned locals that anyone venturing near them, especially after dark, was liable to be shot. 'It is known,' said the *Observer* cryptically, 'there are a number of spies in the Island.' German waiters were rounded up by the army although most of them had long gone before the soldiers got there. Boy Scouts were sent door to door in the Island's towns, asking if there were any foreigners present. Today's Children's Services would have a fit! At Parkhurst, the army arrested a suspicious-looking man carrying maps and charts. It took him several hours to prove that he was a land valuation officer and as patriotic as the next man; one could not be too careful! There were an estimated 35,000 Germans and Austrians in Britain at the outbreak of war. On 5 August the government passed the Aliens Restrictions Act, giving enemy nationals five days to leave. Many did, leaving wives and children behind in some cases. By the end of September 13,600 Germans and Austrians were in internment camps. Throughout the war only twenty-two were convicted of spying, but three of those shot were providing the German government with ship movements in and out of Southampton and Portsmouth.

The most pressing need was for men. The British army on the outbreak of war was small, 247,000 (against the Germans' 864,000) and they were scattered throughout the huge Empire and used to fighting 'small wars' against ill-armed, if determined, natives. The last major European war, in the Crimea, had finished fifty-eight years before and no one, from Field Marshal to Private, had experience of the kind of war that was erupting in Flanders. But in August, the government could still afford to be choosy. For the regular army, a recruit had to be literate, aged between 18 and 25, be at least 5ft 3ins tall with a minimum chest measurement of 34 inches. When Harry Brading of East Cowes volunteered in 1915 he was turned down because he had weak lungs and a glass eye. Traditionally, men served seven years with the Colours and five with the Reserve. The Special Reserve now set up was not so fussy about height and chest measurement and qualifying ages ran from 17 to 35. Ex-soldiers aged between 18 and 42 were particularly welcome.

The Volunteer movement of the 1860s had merged with the Militia and Yeomanry to become the Territorial Army in 1908 and these men would soon find themselves in the Front Line. Princess Beatrice's Isle of Wight Rifles, first raised in a French invasion scare in 1859 was now the 8th Battalion of the Hampshire Regiment and someone took a photograph of them marching up Union Street in Ryde in September 1914. The sun is still shining and the crowds are in their summer whites. Union jacks and Royal Navy ensigns flutter everywhere and the band of the Boy Scouts, in shorts and campaign hats made famous by General Baden Powell in the Boer War, leads the mounted officers and the khaki column.

The tin hats known as 'battle bowlers', the gas capes, the gas masks and the mud are things of the future. It all looks jolly and fun, like the two-week camps on Yaverland Down that the Isle of Wight troop of the Hampshire Yeomanry held each summer. Young men are supposed to thrill to the beat of the drum and the blast of the bugle and dash to the Town Hall or the Drill Hall to enlist. Young women, dewy-eyed, are supposed to let them go. It is something of a cliché now, but it happened and Lord Kitchener's Expeditionary Force, bound for France,

It will all be over by Christmas! The 8th Battalion Hampshire Regiment (IW Rifles) marching up Union Street, Ryde, September 1914.

would depend on them for reinforcements. Across the country, 33,204 men had enlisted 3 September, all of them convinced the war would be short-lived and that God was on their side. Some joined out of genuine patriotic fervour (it was a less cynical age); others for a sense of adventure and excitement. Still others, and this was probably very true of the Isle of Wight, joined the Colours because life on the land was hard, monotonous and unrewarding.

As for the women, the Order of the White Feather was set up. The feather was a traditional symbol of cowardice, exemplified by E W Mason's popular

Hotel Ryde Castle, one of several Island hotels that became convalescent homes to wounded soldiers. *(Trow)*

novel *The Four Feathers* and the girls of 1914 were encouraged to give such a feather to any shirking men they knew. Baroness Orczy is best known today for her novel *The Scarlet Pimpernel* but she also set up, in 1914, the Active Service League. Members were 'never to be seen in public with any man who, being in every way fit and free for service, has refused to respond to his country's call'.

There were 'stirring and touching scenes at Newport railway station' wrote a local reporter as the Royal Fusiliers from the barracks at Albany entrained for the Front. It was a scene being enacted all over the country.

'We have had no actual experience of war of any serious kind since the time of Cromwell,' one local paper letter-writer wrote. 'When and what will be the end of it?'

Adverts in the papers carried the famous challenge – 'Your King and Country Need You. A Call To Arms.'

The Isle of Wight Rifles under the command of Lieutenant Colonel J E Rhodes took over the Island's forts from the Fusiliers as part of Portsmouth's outer defences. Two riflemen were reprimanded because they had been seen lighting cigarettes by torpedo boat crews off the coast. This sort of thing would become part of the folklore of the Second World War.

The Warwickshire Regiment, stationed on the Island, went on board a Red Star liner moored off Yarmouth and arrested five Austrians working as stewards. They were frogmarched to Golden Hill Fort and Parkhurst Barracks, apparently 'quite pleased with their lot'. Northwood House in Cowes and the Castle Hotel in Ryde opened up as troop hospitals as did a number of the Island's manor houses – Swainston, Gatcombe, Afton and Winchester House in Lake.

Football and other sporting clubs were badly hit by the volunteers queuing to 'do their bit'. In fact, various clubs seemed to try to outdo each other with numbers of recruits. Ventnor Cricketers did well; so did Seaview Sports Syndicate. Funds were set up by the great and good of the Island, one pledged to knitting woolly sweaters which were not part of the kit doled out to the new Tommies. Charitable organizations like this were dominated by upper middle class ladies, many of whom are mentioned by name in the local Press. Working class women were too busy surviving, especially those with their men away. Many volunteers would not need their 'jumpers' for months. Mobilization was a slow process and many men found themselves wearing 'Kitchener blue' rather than khaki and going on route marches with yard-brooms over their shoulders.

Almost immediately there was an opportunistic criminal element which set to work. Ernest Vaughan and George Spragg of Newport were convicted of stealing khaki cloth, the price of which was soaring. The courts became fixated on alien residents, like Captain F W van Herbert, a military writer from Shanklin who was not only a British subject but had been decorated in the Boer War fourteen years earlier.

The recruiting campaign was in full swing by the end of September, with speeches, flags and bands. 'It is not so much your duty to take your place in the firing line,' said W D Garrison of the Royal Colonial Institute, 'as your exalted privilege' and the editor of the *Observer* talked about this 'wonderful war'. With deep irony in the context of what was to come, he wrote of 'the astonishing rapidity and continuity of action'. By October, the war had ground

An infantry detachment in Monkton Street, Ryde, probably in the summer of 1915.

to a stalemate in the mud of Flanders. Adverts appeared in all Island papers. One showed Britannia addressing men – 'Will you fight for your king and country or will you skulk in the safety your fathers won and your brothers are struggling to maintain?' It all worked; the IW Rifles had an extra 800 men by October and the Wessex (Howitzer) Royal Field Artillery had been brought up to strength.

The large number of troops stationed in Island forts (and in some cases foisted on individuals) caused problems. The billeting budget for 1914 provided for 9d[1] for each soldier per night. Breakfast allowance was 7$^1/_2$d, dinner (lunch) 1s 7$^1/_2$d and supper 4$^1/_2$d. The notion of three meals a day was not one that all recruits were used to. Week after week there were cases of drunkenness and punch ups between these soldiers, which involved the police and the civilian courts. Andrew Olsen, a Norwegian sailor, was fined for disorderly conduct in George Street in Ryde. Thomas Thornton of the Royal Warwickshire Regiment received one month's hard labour for sexually assaulting six-year-old Winifred Chiverton at Freshwater. It seems odd today that the little victim should be named, but the opening years of the 20th century had yet to see a move towards protecting children. In fact, the huge casualty rate of 1914-18 made children a precious commodity for the first time – they had to fill the gap created by the 'lost generation'. A six-year-old boy, Harry Exell, was killed when he was run over by a wagon of the 2nd South Midland Brigade of the Royal Field Artillery on Hunnyhill in Newport.

Blackout regulations were brought in by October and continued to cause problems for the duration of the war. Not as draconian as those imposed by the Second World War, they nevertheless were part of DORA (Defence Of the Realm Acts) which saw the government assume sweeping powers which were totally at odds with the non-interventionist doctrine of the previous century. The street lights suddenly went out completely in Ryde on the first Tuesday in October because the Portsmouth naval authorities feared zeppelin raids. In fact the zeppelin was *the* terror weapon of the Great War and was feared as gas was feared twenty years later. There *were* zeppelin raids later, over London and the east coast, but nothing serious happened in the Isle of Wight. That said, there were zeppelin sightings. Raymond Saunders of the 2/8th Company, Royal Engineers, was stationed at Horse Sands Fort (one of Palmerston's Follies in the Solent) and on Portsdown Hill overlooking Portsmouth Naval Base. The place was a maze of eerie tunnels and he turned his searchlight onto one of the lumbering silent killers one night in October 1915. There were to be no fireworks on Bonfire Night this year and somebody suggested that Boy Scouts could be used as link men, to guide people home after dark with torches.

---

1. The currency of course was LSD – pounds, shillings and pence. For younger readers, there were 20 shillings in the pound and 12 pence in a shilling. Frequently, goods cost half a crown (2s 6d) or a tanner (6d).

The *County Press* was the best known Island newspaper and was sent out to men in the Trenches. The first war casualty, Bandsman Edmund Belcher, died on the pavement here after a gas main blew up on 17 October 1914. *(Trow)*

Local firms were quick to capitalise on the situation. Allenby's powdered milk was pure and rich and 'especially valuable for the feeding of our Wounded and Invalid Soldiers and Sailors'. It was available in tins costing 1/6d, 3s and 6s.

The first Island casualty of the war took place on 17 October. It was a Saturday night and a huge explosion ripped through the pavement outside the *County Press* offices near Newport's market place. There were panicked shouts of 'Zeppelin!' and shopkeepers put their lights out. Some witnesses were convinced they had seen aircraft overhead and the bang was heard a mile away. In fact, it was a common or garden gas explosion and Bandsman Edmund Belcher of the IW Rifles who had been passing by was killed by a manhole cover that crushed him as it fell.

It was in October that letters sent by soldiers to family and friends in the Island began to be published in the *County Press*. The paper may have been taking a risk by publishing these, but probably by October the letters themselves would have been censored with the blue pencil of officers at the Front. Lance Corporal Jack Ryall, the son of an ex-police sergeant, who was serving with the King's Royal Rifles 'somewhere in France' wrote:

'I received your letters safe and two *County Press*. Smoking gives you a lot of comfort when you are in the trenches ... While I have been here I have seen the finest and also the saddest sights of my life. ... I had a letter from Aunt Charlotte and she said "Poor little Jack. I don't expect you can smile now like you used to" ... Remember me to little Will and tell him not to worry about Kaiser Bill. When we go into Berlin we will smoke him out.'

By this time the 'minor inconveniences' of the Home Front were beginning to grow. No bands played in the seaside towns and the visitors who had left in droves in the summer showed no sign of returning. Communication with the mainland was badly disrupted and people in Ryde complained of the Portsmouth naval searchlights that 'play havoc with the pattern on the wallpaper in our bed-rooms throughout the night'. Dim red lights in shops were thought preferable to green – people all looked ill under those. Most people kept the moaning to themselves, no doubt considering it unpatriotic to do otherwise. The editor of the *County Press* wrote:

'In ordinary times, the faddist, the crank and the grumbler will wage a battle royal over things of this category, yet in these days he deems it wise and consistent to hold his peace.'

There was already a paper shortage by the end of the year and the *County Press* was only available on demand. This would worsen as the war went on. The government even had a special official, the Paper Controller, whose offices were at Buckingham Gate in London. Ironically, newspaper circulation increased, both in the Island and nationally, because people naturally wanted to know how the war was going. The cost of paper was going up however and some magazines did not survive 1918.

Recruiting and fund raising went on as before. The Island Branch of the RSPCA held an Animal Day – 'Please buy a flower and help Animals at the Front and at Home'. The British army relied on horses. 'I won't say horses won the war for us,' wrote Gunner Fred Lloyd of the Royal Field Artillery, 'but we would never have won it without them.' Jack Seely and his famous horse Warrior became icons of gallantry in the Isle of Wight and France where they fought, but horses were not used just by the cavalry. Guns were pulled by them, as were munitions wagons, food supplies and ambulances. The Belgians harnessed dogs to pull their guns and at least 100,000 carrier pigeons were used to send messages during the war; 95 per cent of them reached their destination.

Thirteen members of the Ryde Gaslight Company joined up and the advertisements continued to bully and cajole. A smiling sergeant (now *there* was a rarity!) assured hopefuls – 'There's a place for you, my lad!' The Motor Ambulance Fund set up in Ryde raised £235 6s 6d in a week. H Pack and Co

Soldiers of the King. Khaki had been the official colour of service uniforms since 1898. Buttons on most Other Ranks tunics carried the royal coat of arms. Only the cap badges denoted a distinctive unit, as well as letters on the shoulder straps. A cavalryman or Horse Artilleryman was recognizable by his spurs. The two men pictured here spoke highly of 'Galloper Jack' Seely and his Canadian cavalry. *(Flux)*

IN·MEMORIAM
HALLAM·LORD·TENNYSON
BORN·AUGUST·11·1852· DIED· DECEMBER·2·1928
G.C.M.G.·P.C.·LITT.D.·D.C.L.
GRAND·CROSS·OF·THE·ORDER·OF·THE·RISING·SUN
D.L.·J.P.·HANTS·DEP·GOV·ISLE·OF·WIGHT
GOV·AND·C·IN·C·SOUTH·AUSTRALIA·1899·1902
GOV·GEN·OF·COMMONWEALTH·OF·AUSTRALIA·1902·1904
SON·OF·ALFRED·LORD·TENNYSON.

MORTUA VIVESCUNT.

ALSO·IN·LOVING·MEMORY·OF
ALFRED·AUBREY·TENNYSON
SECOND·SON·OF·HALLAM·LORD·TENNYSON·AND·AUDREY·LADY·TENNYSON
CAPTAIN·9TH·BATTALION·RIFLE·BRIGADE·AND·ON·STAFF
SERVED·IN·FRANCE, BELGIUM·AND·THE·BALKANS.
BORN·2ND·MAY·1891,
KILLED·IN·ACTION·AT·FLEURY·LE·MARTEL
23RD·MARCH·1918.
WE·DOUBT·NOT·THAT·FOR·ONE·SO·TRUE
THERE·MUST·BE·OTHER·NOBLER·WORK·TO·DO.

One of the most famous names of the West Wight was that of Alfred, Lord Tennyson, Victoria's poet laureate. This marble tomb in St John's Church, Freshwater, commemorates the poet's son Hallam and his grandson Alfred Aubrey of the Rifle Brigade who was killed at Fleury le Martel 23 March 1918. *(Trow)*

were selling mufflers in khaki, navy and grey and the *Observer* offices had the newest designs in mourning cards. The Victorian cult of death, with black mourning clothes, ostrich plumes and macabre tombstones had all but vanished by 1914 as had the spiritualism often associated with it. While soldiers on leave sometimes wore single black crepe armbands on their left sleeves as a mark of respect, widows and mothers still wore full black, at least in the weeks following a loss. Such was the casualty rate at the Front that more people turned to mediums and Spritualist churches than at any time since the 1850s.

By and large, recruitment followed class patterns. Most officers came from the public schools and the aristocracy lost more men in 1914-18 than at any time since the Wars of the Roses. The tendency was for these men to refer to the enemy as the 'Hun' or the 'Boche'. The Other Ranks came traditionally from the working class; they called Germans 'Jerry' or 'Fritz'. A letter to his mother written by Beryl Flux's uncle, who served in the Royal Horse Artillery, said, 'I was looking forward to sending you some violets [from France] as they were on the point of blossoming when we had to move in case Fritz should attempt an advance.' 'Kraut' was an Americanism not heard until 1918.

A German bullet was no respecter of rank or status. Among the casualty lists put up in the Island Post Offices and printed in the newspapers was Prince Maurice of Battenburg, son of Princess Henry, better known generally as Princess Beatrice, the Island's governor and Alfred Aubrey Tennyson, the grandson of the former poet laureate who lived at Farringford.

Lists of benefactors to a dozen different funds appeared weekly in the Press along with the amount donated. One donor paid £50 and 'a promise of £5 per month for six months, should the war last so long.'

By December it was clear that the war would indeed last longer than most had anticipated. 'After three months of the war the outlook is by no means lacking in hopelessness ...' said the editor of the *Observer*, a far cry from the unbridled optimism of August. In what looked like xenophobic desperation, Belgians living on the Island were forced to leave, even though we had gone to war to defend 'gallant little Belgium' in the first place. This bit of mean-spiritedness seems at odds with the general mood of the country, at least as far as Fleet Street was concerned. The National Press were full of praise for the plucky Belgians and people (no doubt Islanders among them) bought the fund-raising King Albert's Book in vast numbers.

Bridge parties, so beloved of the middle classes, were in decline with increasing numbers away at the Front and, to show support for her new husband, Hilda Nash of High Park, Ryde, got married in khaki. We shall come across other examples of weddings later, but there was a general increase in matrimony, especially in 1915-16 when only single men were expected to enlist. There was something of the 'live while you may' attitude seen more sharply in the Second World War and courtships were often whirlwind. Raymond Saunders, on watch for zeppelins on Horse Sands Fort, married a former servant who worked at the Maypole grocer's shop in Portsmouth in 1915.

Christmas card from the belongings of Wilfred Joliffe. Soldiers at the Front received regular mail, especially those in France – letters and cards usually took three or four days to arrive. (Greenham)

A Ryde woman, Mabel Bartlett, had just got back after two years in Germany by early December. Propaganda in Berlin claimed that London was in total darkness, Tommies were running away from Germans along the Front and the recruiting system had broken down. Various friends Mabel had made assured her

In memory of Mark Leigh Goldie, Major V. Battery R.H.A. M.V.O. D.S.O. who died of wounds in France March 1915 aged 36yrs and of his brother Amyas Leigh Goldie Gloucester Regt attd 4th Worcesters who fell in action in Gallipoli Aug 1915 aged 36yrs. Nature might stand up and say to all the world that these were men.

Wealthy families often had elaborate memorials for their dead loved ones. This one, in bright enamel colours, comes from Shorwell Church and shows St George, the patron saint of England, standing over a slain dragon. The memorial is to two brothers of the Goldie family – Amyas, who was killed at Gallipoli with the Gloucester Regiment in August 1915 and Mark, of V Battery, Royal Horse Artillery, who died of wounds, March 1915. *(Trow)*

that they would see her in London by Christmas. Advertisements offered excellent Christmas presents for men on active service – vacuum flasks, wire-cutters and knives that opened tins. Undoubtedly the most famous present of that first Christmas was Princess Mary's Gift Box. The princess was seventeen at the time and spearheaded a fundraising campaign to send comforts to the troops exactly as her great grandmother, Victoria, had done in the Boer War. These little brass boxes (there are still thousands of them in existence) contained tobacco or cigarettes, a pipe and lighter or sweets and chocolate.

The famous unofficial 'truce' of Christmas 1914 was described by Rifleman Mallard of the Machine Gun Section of the Rifle Brigade. There was a Christmas tree with candles on top of a German trench and both sides emerged from their dug outs to talk by searchlight, shaking hands and exchanging knickknacks. The Germans were using British-made matches and the Tommies shared their tea and cocoa, tasting it first to let the Germans know it was not poisoned. 'They are very "cute" boys,' Mallard wrote, 'most of them very young.' They sang songs to each other from their respective trenches but just after

Princess Mary's gift box, issued to every serving soldier, sailor and airman at Christmas 1914. Headed Imperium Britannicum (the British Empire) it also carried a list of Allies – Belgium, France, Russia, Japan, Serbia and, slightly bizarrely, to modern eyes Montenegro. *(Trow)*

midnight on Christmas Day, the shelling started again. Rifleman Mallard was keeping a couple of German cigars for his father, when the war was over.

By that Christmas, Germany's Schlieffen plan, the attempt to take Paris and knock France out of the war before the Russians could mobilize, lay in tatters. The British Expeditionary Force had held the Germans at Mons and the French under Marshal Joffre had counter-attacked along the Marne. The war of movement had become a war of stalemate. Pounded by deadly heavy artillery at long range, both sides dug trenches and stayed put, waiting for winter to pass as armies had done for centuries and planning for a spring offensive. The fact that the British Expeditionary Force and the French held on to Ypres meant that the Channel ports remained open for more volunteers to be landed. Trench warfare has been described as 90 per cent routine and 10 per cent terror. Most units served for five days in the Front Line (Fire) trenches, protected by sandbags and barbed wire. Five days were then spent in the maze of support trenches, never far from the Front. Here, men had to be ready to go forward at a moment's notice in the event of an enemy attack. The next five days were safer, but men were often used to bring supplies to the forward trench system.

The lighter side of war. Fred Kingswell's 34th Squadron had, in common with many units, musicians and 'turns' quite happy to put on drag for the amusements of the lads in the rest areas behind the lines. The show was Cinderella (extreme left – isn't 'she' gorgeous?)
(Yates)

'Terror stalks through Christendom,' wrote the editor of the *Observer*. 'There is grief and mourning in thousands of homes and millions of our men are marching or lying in their trenches, determined to kill or be killed.'

'Are we downhearted?' Well, perhaps just a little.

Chapter Two

1915

'Stand in the trench, Achilles,
Flame-capped, and shout for me.'[2]

THE HORROR OF trench warfare was brought home to Mr and Mrs Thomas of Leed Street, Shanklin by their son, Fred, who was serving with the 8th Hussars, part of the 3rd Cavalry Brigade of the Indian Expeditionary Force. The cavalry were learning the hard way that their arm was largely redundant and yet one of the biggest bills facing the British government in the Great War was for horse fodder. 'One poor fellow in the next trench,' Thomas wrote, 'said he would have one last shot at the Germans before he was relieved. A bullet split his head open. Another one was taken out of the trench with both legs and arms blown off by a shell.' This was printed by the *County Press* and left the 'weary Willies' and 'tired Tims' still at home in no doubt about the realities of modern war. The

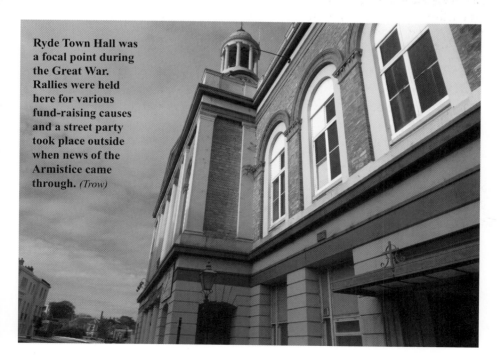

Ryde Town Hall was a focal point during the Great War. Rallies were held here for various fund-raising causes and a street party took place outside when news of the Armistice came through. *(Trow)*

2. *Untitled* Patrick Shaw-Stewart, Naval Division, killed in France 1917.

trenches had been dug by the 230,000 miners who now found themselves in khaki. The soil of Flanders was soft and trenches often collapsed. German trenches tended to be deeper and more solid than those of the Allies.

The Oxford historian A F Pollard gave a talk at Ryde's Town Hall in January in which he hoped 'May 1915 witness the downfall of the King's enemies, as decisively as 1815 – that is the Happy New Year we want and pray for.' He was referring to Waterloo a hundred years earlier and the overthrow of another tyrant in the Kaiser's mould – Napoleon Bonaparte.

Costs of everything were going up against the backdrop of German 'bestiality' and zeppelins were hitting East Anglia and the Yorkshire coast. Two weeks before Christmas of the previous year, 1500 shells had been fired by the German High Seas Fleet at the seaside towns of Scarborough and Whitby, killing 127 people, perhaps a foretaste of what was to come for Sandown and Shanklin. Zeppelins had hit Lowestoft and Great Yarmouth. A satirical version of John Hassell's famous holiday poster about Skegness being so bracing showed a salty sea dog skipping along the beach as shells burst at his feet. In the event of an aerial attack on Island towns, the church bells were to be rung; in Ryde, specifically, those of All Saints, Holy Trinity and Swanmore. In East Cowes, the shipbuilding firm of JS White would sound a series of sharp blasts on their works' hooters. The public should go into their cellars and basements, although such an event was unlikely – twenty five years later, of course, it was standard practice.

Ever anxious to cash in on the situation – although actual war-profiteering was made a crime – local chemists in Ryde and Brading offered Samphos for the nerves and quoted the ex-Surgeon-General of the army who warned that 'thousands of people are at this moment unconsciously approaching a breakdown.' Happy days! German prisoners were rumoured to be held in prison ships in the Solent. The *Canada*, the *Tunisian* and the *Andania* were anchored off Ryde as the year turned. The *Tunisian* had been a troopship in the Boer War. Neither the *Canada* nor the *Andania* would survive 1914-18. The curious could inspect a German helmet called a *pickelhaub* which was on display in a Ryde tobacconist's window. These helmets, later replaced by the more practical *stalhelm*, were particularly prized as war souvenirs by men coming home on leave.

Throughout the early spring, more special constables were sworn in. Ryde for example only had a ten-man force of regular policemen and only three of these were between 20 and 40 years of age. One of the new men was W Player-Brigstocke, a JP for the county whose grandfather had ridden the Charge of the Heavy Brigade at Balaclava in the Crimean War. Gentlemen like him were targeted in the on-going recruiting advertisements – 'Have *you* a butler, groom, chauffeur, gardener or gamekeeper serving you who at the moment should be serving his King and Country?' For more humble beings, another advert asked, 'Do *you* feel happy as you walk along the streets and see other men wearing the King's uniform? If not why don't you enlist today and do your share?' The recruiting office in Castle Street, Newport, stood ready and open.

Interspersed with all this, papers carried strident editorials on the appalling immorality of the Germans; the 'beastly Hun' were murdering women and children. Some of this was genuine. German troops streaming into Belgium back in September were ordered to inflict *Schrecklichkeit* (frightfulness). Poster artists and cartoonists continued to depict Fritz as fat, shaven-headed, moronic and half-man, half-beast.

The cranks of course continued, as they always will, to write letters to the editor. Why, oh why, had we not persevered with a Channel tunnel to transport reinforcements quickly and safely to the Front? And could it be true that the unusually heavy rainfall in March was linked to the firing of the big guns across

'Men Who March Away'. These soldiers are on their way to the station at an unknown Island town. Locals saw them off whenever possible, but many of the troops stationed in the Island were not local, merely passing through. *(Downer)*

that very Channel? Lord Kitchener, whose recruiting poster face had made him a household celebrity had said that he expected the war to last three years. Most islanders could not, apparently, accept that.

Editors were in no doubt that artillery was going to win the war and there would be 'brilliant victory' over the bloodthirsty, monomaniac Kaiser. There were one or two warning voices. Dr Charles Myers claimed that prolonged exposure to shelling affects smell, sight and taste and could induce hysteria. Shell-shock was a new phenomenon of this war, if only because of the sheer size of the conflict and the nature of high explosive bombardment. The high command certainly had no patience with it – the 306 men in the British army shot for cowardice in the Great War only received a grudging pardon from Tony Blair's government in 2006. Gilbert Frankau summed it up superbly with his poem *The Deserter*:

'Fire!' called the Sergeant-Major.
The muzzles flamed as he spoke;
And the shameless soul of a nameless man
Went up in the cordite-smoke.[3]

Meanwhile, the recruiting campaigns jolted the consciences of fathers – 'Daddy,' a little boy asks his father, 'why weren't *you* a soldier during the war?' 'Join the army at once and help to secure the glorious Empire of which your little son will be a citizen.'

Gas was used for the first time by the Germans at the second battle of Ypres. This was contrary to the Hague Convention which had drawn up rules for 'civilized' warfare; it merely proved the on-going barbarism of the 'Kultur' of the Germans, but of course, the Allies had to use gas in retaliation.

By May, amid Belgian soldiers' reports that British POWs were being badly treated by their German captors, the government, particularly Winston Churchill at the Admiralty, launched the ill-conceived and pointless Gallipoli campaign. The idea was to free the Straits of the Dardanelles, take Constantinople (Istanbul) and knock Turkey out of the war. This would free up pressure on the Russians who were floundering in the East and enable an Allied attack on Austria from the south. The initial idea of this being a naval campaign had to be abandoned because of the unknown number of mines in the Straits, so the army had to be sent in to take the Gallipoli peninsula.

This book is not about the specific military actions of Island men in the Great War, but the events at Gallipoli became seared into the minds of the Isle of Wight Rifles so a special mention must be made of them.

In May, the Rifles were ordered to the St Albans area where they trained for two months, marching in full pack at the fast light infantry pace. At Bury St Edmunds, on their first night there, six zeppelins came over and dropped fifty

3. Gilbert Frankau, Captain, Royal Artillery

pound bombs that flattened the Queen's Head Hotel and several shops. The Rifles were called out quell a riot in the town and save a German pub landlord from being lynched!

On 30 July the Rifles left Liverpool on board the *Aquitania*, passed Gibraltar on 2 August and reached Mudros four days later. From here they were transferred to smaller craft and sailed for Imbros before being landed in barges on the sandy beaches of Suvla Bay. The first sight Islanders had of actual war was of some two and a half thousand men with shattered limbs and ripped bodies being evacuated to base hospitals that could not cope with the numbers involved.

The Rifles received their own baptism of fire on 12 August, the day, ironically, that grouse shooting opened in the Scottish Highlands. They were ordered forward across rough country and a salt marsh that ended in the Anafarta Ridge, a series of dunes and hillocks, heavily defended by Turkish machine-gun emplacements. 'My God,' Captain Clayton Ratsey, the son of a boat-building family from Cowes muttered to a fellow officer, 'we'll all be

The plaque on the Drill Hall wall in Newport, commemorating the establishment of Princess Beatrice's Isle of Wight Rifles in 1860. As part of the Volunteer movement, the unit's principal job was to protect the Island from a possible French invasion. *(Trow)*

A naval shell, covered with successive layers of green paint, marks the corner of the parade ground at the Newport Drill Hall. The Island's oldest cinema, the Rink, showing films during the Great War, was nearby. *(Trow)*

killed.' He was nearly right. He died along with over 300 Islanders that day. Another who died later was Albert Downer, 23, of a Methodist family from Calbourne. He had joined the Rifles before the war and his father was out hedging on the Fulholding Farm Estate where he was bailiff when one of his daughters brought the dreaded telegram. Albert had been polishing his boots on 31 October when a sniper's bullet found him. Ironically, that was the day that the general commanding in Gallipoli, finally decided that the campaign was useless and asked permission to pull out.

The following may not be great poetry, but it deserves its place in a book about the Isle of Wight in the Great War –

'Let us tell how the Island Rifles,
Eight hundred of the best,
Crossed Anafarta Valley
To Anafarta's Crest.
And how their trusty leader,
Colonel Rhodes the brave,
Dashed through the Turkish valley

Trophies of the Isle of Wight Rifles. It is unknown when or where this photograph was taken but the ship emblem of the unit can clearly be recognised at the top of the trophy shield. Many units played each other at sports in peace time and medals and cups were presented to the winners. *(Downer)*

To victory or the grave.
It is a famous story,
Proclaim it far and wide
And the Island's children
Re-echo it with pride,
How Princess Beatrice's Rifles
Their name for ever made,
When they stormed Anafarta Valley
In the One Six Third Brigade.
It was on the twelfth of August
That the order, it came through,
That the 163rd Brigade
Its duty had to do.
Our officers nobly led us
As we went to face the foe.

Alas, our valiant major fell
And some gallant captains too.
Norfolks, Suffolks, Hampshires
Formed that brigade so brave
And they fought like true Britons,
Many finding a soldier's grave.
Praise to our fighting parson
And to doctor Raymond too,
For their devotion to the wounded
While around the bullets flew.
Now remember the Island rifles
Who faced death on that far shore,
Some called them the last hope of England
But they won't call them that any more,
For their names are engraved at Gallipoli,
With Anzac staunch and true,
Their deeds shall shine in history
Showing what Island men can do.
Yes, it is a famous story.
Proclaim it far and wide
And let the Island children
Re-echo it with pride,
How our Princess's Rifles
Faced fearful odds that day
And won undying glory
In the great Gallipoli fray.'[4]

The evacuation happened smoothly on the night of 15 December but Turkey remained in the war and the Dardanelles untaken. For years afterwards, the incoming tides along the peninsula brought with them human bones, the testimony of war's folly. In the eight months of the campaign, there were 57,000 Allied dead, of whom 34,000 were British and the rest largely Anzacs (Australians and New Zealanders). The Turks lost 65,000 with a further 110,000 wounded. The Anzacs won a special place in the hearts of Britain for their dogged heroism, even if their laid-back attitude horrified the more staid elements of the British officer class. The feeling was not always mutual, however. Although they generally got on well with the Scots regiments, most Aussies shared the view of one Tasmanian in 1916 – 'Pommie Jackeroos and just as hopeless ... most of them crawlers or favourites of some toff.'

As the year wore on at home, realisation dawned that tourism, the Island's lifeblood, had all but dried up. The Island was a rural community, the only

**RMS *Lusitania* heads out into the Atlantic ocean and her
meeting with destiny.**

serious industry geared largely
to boat building, concentrated
at Cowes. Tourism had begun
tentatively in the 1820s and
received a huge boost with the
royal connection of Victoria
and Albert at Osborne after 1845
and the arrival of the railways after 1862. Now, 'in the Year of Your Lord
1915'[5] it was rumoured that the Island was a fortress surrounded by barbed wire.
To counter this, Admiral Earl Jellicoe, who had long had Island associations,
printed posters that said that the Isle of Wight 'is the safest place in the world'.

The sinking of the passenger ship, the *Lusitania*, was seen as a new low in the
bestiality of the Germans and anti-German riots in London had their pale echoes
in the Island – eggs were thrown at visiting Americans because they were of
German or Austrian birth. The *Lusitania* was a Cunard liner that was hit by a
single torpedo fired from *Kapitan-Leutnant* Walter Schweiger's U20 submarine
in May. 1201 people died, including 94 children and the ship sank in eighteen

5. John Drinkwater *Nineteen-Fifteen*, 1915

minutes. There were 128 Americans on board.

And another rumour was spreading too – The *Observer*'s editor wrote,

'It would be a pity after the voluntary system has yielded such splendid results, if conscription should be necessary, but the possibility must be faced.'

Recruiting continued to be a vital priority. 'Standing on the corner smoking fags,' the adverts warned, 'will not beat the Germans.'

By 1915 it was clear that the numbers volunteering for the army would not be enough. In October the Derby scheme was introduced by which men aged 18 to 41 'attested', that is, agreed to enlist when asked to do so. These men became 'armleteers', wearing khaki armbands with a scarlet crown to show their readiness to serve. One Islander who attested was Archer Brading of Verona, Maresfield Rd, East Cowes, on 6 December 1915. His attestation card has survived – 'The above named man has been attested and transferred to the Army Reserve until required for service.' Unfortunately, J S White, for whom Brading worked, were not happy with this and told him to stay put! For married men, there was a separation allowance, brought in on 1 March. Wages for men with wives increased to 12s 6d. 21 shillings was paid for a wife and two children and there was 2s for each extra child. Whereas officers were often earning less than they had been before 1914, for many enlisted men these payments were a godsend. A meeting at the Church Institute at St Helens late in May spoke of setting up an Isle of Wight Company of the Royal Engineers or a Portsmouth 'Pals' battalion. Other towns and cities went down this route, with predictably tragic results. The idea was sound – men who had been friends since boyhood sharing the privations of campaign and the dangers of battle. But in reality, as Liverpool and Birmingham found out to their cost, a single shell in a single trench could wipe out much of the young manhood of an entire district. Like so much else dreamed up by men who never saw a shot fired in anger, it had not been thought through.

News was still a two-way street in the summer of 1915. Letters, postcards and Island newspapers, posted for example from a specified building in Ryde's Union Street, reached the trenches of France and even, eventually, Gallipoli. Most parcels got to France in four days and foodstuffs were usually distributed between friends when they arrived. And of course, letters kept coming from the Front, although by now, soldiers were warned not to give specific details. Private Phil Gilbert wrote to his sister 'Miss Popsie Wopsie Gilbert, "Songster"' at Glengary, Albert St, Ventnor. This was late June 1915 and he was still at Watford, training. His witty address is –

No change –

Yet –

Watfor(d) –

Don't Know –

Philip Gilbert. Studio portraits like this were very popular, mostly taken in towns in France and Belgium and sent back to loved ones. This one is unusually relaxed and shows the youth of many of the 'Tommies' in the Great War. *(Boxall)*

'Oh, I would give anything, bar my soul, to be at Ventnor now and for ever more amen.' The Gilberts kept a bakery in the town and Phil had been to a Wesleyan chapel in Watford which took him back to his childhood. The girls in the choir there were better-looking than at Ventnor and had better voices; one of them sang a solo – 'Land of Hopeless Glory' and, perhaps oddly, the Russian national anthem – 'it knocks our anthem into a cocked hat.' He wanted a weekend pass to get home to see the rambler rose in his garden at home in all its glory. He feigns outrage that his sister had given away some of his clothes to the Belgian refugee cause – 'So after the war you mean me to go about in the nude! I have never heard of such a thing! I can see you don't expect me to come back alive so you had better order the oak case and brass fittings in double-quick time.'

His gallows humour had gone by 19 July when he wrote his will. It was addressed simply 'To Mother. Private. To be opened after news of my death.' There are still traces of sealing wax on the back of the envelope.

'If I am knocked over I want the following belongings of mine to be distributed. To my dear Mother I am afraid none of my things would be of any use, so I ask her to accept the knowledge that I died for the king and the old country and a very sincere love and respect for her. What more could a Mother wish from a son?

Pops – thermos flask that Uncle Will gave me

Jack – all my books including the Harmsworth Popular Science

Basil – telescope and drawing instruments

Ruth – fountain pen with which I write this; should it be in working order

Bet – writing case after letters which it contains have been burnt

Ethel – anything else not mentioned.

Any money due from the military authorities to Mother who might want to put it into the business – I think this is all I have to give.'

The other thing was his life. Rifleman 1709 Philip Gilbert of the 1/8th Battalion, the Hampshire Regiment was one of the 300 who died on 12 August in Gallipoli. He was nineteen.

A friend of his, Arthur Watson of Upton Road, Ryde, died the same day. In his last letter home, written two days earlier, he wrote, 'They are just allowing us to write a short letter before we start off – to show the Turks what the IW Rifles are made of.' They were made of flesh and bone. 'Please God, I shall come through all right, but if not, you must take it as being for the best. May I come through safe to see you all again.'

With bad news like this coming through week after week, M V Hawkins of Ryde was moved to write to his local paper –

'I have seen some very bad cases of wounded coming from the trenches

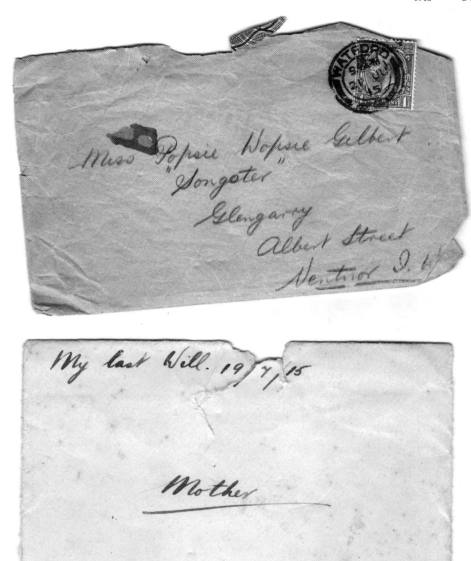

Sad mementoes. The letter addressed to his sister 'Miss Popsie Wopsie' Gilbert by her brother from Watford on his way to the Front. The other envelope contains the Rifleman's will and carries a misprint which may have been the result of emotion – the word 'after' appears twice. *(Boxall)*

British troops on Gully Beach awaiting evacuation. Turkish shells are exploding in the sea and these men seem unperturbed.

and when one reads of men at home at Woolwich Arsenal ... going on strike, it makes one feel devilish wild.'

Munitions workers could be found in various shipyards in the Island and their numbers were augmented by 'northerners' by 1916, but the major cities now had them in their thousands. In some cases, their numbers were already supplemented by women since manpower losses caused by so many volunteering had to be made up somehow. These women, whose skin turned so yellow with handling TNT that they were called 'canaries', earned half what men did for the same work. Many people – and various manufacturers were happy to agree – thought that married women should work unpaid because otherwise they were 'taking bread out of the mouths of the poor'. The lighter National Press called them Munitionettes. In those factories, as well as in the coal mines of South Wales and the North, conditions were appalling as ever greater output was demanded. Accidents occurred in both work places on a scale previously unknown, but most people shared Hawkins' view that anywhere at Home was a 'cushy number' by comparison with the Trenches. The Minister of Munitions, in a speech made in 1915, said, 'We must keep striking, striking, striking.' D S MacColl, one of the lesser war poets wrote 'The Miners' Response' –

'We do; the present desperate stage
Of fighting brings us luck;
And in the higher war we wage
(For higher wage) *We struck.*'

There was no doubt that iron and steel bosses, coal-owners and many farmers did well out of the war, increasing their profits because what they had to sell was much in demand. This was not readily passed on to the workers and Herbert Asquith's government turned a blind eye.

Specific recruiting now began in earnest. The Royal Engineers needed horse drivers. Only men with experience were required. They had to be 5ft 3 inches to 5ft 7 inches (the ideal height for cavalry generally) and be under 40 years of age. A poet joined in with the general air of patriotism which still prevailed –

'They told the Spartan woman long ago,
Her son had fallen as he faced the foe.
"Then bury him," she said, with steadfast face,
"And let the younger brother take his place".'

The Isle of Wight is full of war memorials today of brothers who died in the same conflict, the same 'big push', the same trench.

The editor of the *Observer* wrote,

'We are not the same people to outward seeing, as we were a year ago. We have passed from idle over-confidence, through anxious despondency, to a calm and steadfast and characteristic resolve at all costs to see this thing through.'

To Private William Walker of the Warwickshire Regiment, it did not look as though William Smith had that resolve because he was not wearing uniform and he assaulted him in the street. 'Perhaps I was in uniform,' Smith told his attacker, 'when you were a boy.' His wife, with him at the time, had just received news of her brother's death at the Front. Walker got fourteen days hard labour.

The memorial to the dead of Havenstreet. Three members of the Salmon family are included here. *(Trow)*

The first anniversary of the start of the war, on 4 August, saw a huge patriotic meeting outside the Theatre Royal in Ryde. It was all a great struggle for liberty and the Island had done well for volunteers. It could do better still. The wounded were coming in to Hazelwood, a large house in Haylands on the edge of Ryde and concerts were held there regularly and at the Island's hospitals to keep up the men's morale. These concerts, featuring troupes of strolling players, were reported in detail each week by Island papers, as examples of the war's 'feel-good factors'.

Morale was beginning to be a problem, even before the news of the Rifles at Suvla Bay came through. David Arnott, aged 60, from Ryde, killed himself after he had read the newspapers – 'The Russians are gone; God help us all.' It may be that Mr Arnott was more prescient than most because the Russians had not gone – yet. Against the Austrians they scored some successes, but against the better trained and equipped Germans lost every time. Revolutionary forces inside Russia may well have been planning the overthrow of the Tsar, Nicholas II, but the revolution itself would not take place until March 1917 and even then the Russian war effort continued for eight months.

In the meantime, the *Isle of Wight Observer* kept up the anti-German pressure with comparative crime figures from the two countries. Between 1897 and 1910, there were 97 murders in Britain; 350 in Germany. In Britain there were 216 rapes compared with 9,381 in Germany. 1262 people were wounded in Britain, whereas 172,453 Germans suffered that fate. As for incest, the figures for Britain totted up to 56 as opposed to 573 for Germany. In the last example, the paper was cheating. Incest was not a crime at all in Britain until 1908.

There was no allusion to the terrible Gallipoli summer but at the end of August, a month that saw tourism all but disappear, it was possible to see a special short film at the Island's Ryde cinema showing the IW Rifles leaving Watford for who-knew-where. It was produced by Harold Shaw and had an all star cast including Mr Henry Ainsley. The poet Henry Newbolt, famous for his patriotic poetry before the war had reservations about such films.

'O living pictures of the dead,
O songs without a sound,
O fellowship whose phantom tread
Hallows a phantom ground –
How in a gleam have these revealed
The faith we have not found.'[6]

Throughout the war, films of all descriptions, not merely propaganda like this one were shown to enthusiastic audiences. They were silent of course, with captions and appropriate organ-playing and were so popular that it was sensible to book to be sure of a seat. Some Island cinemas (the first to be opened was The Rink in Newport) entertained the audience during reel changes with comic turns. Little Lady Little, less than two feet tall, would cavort on the balcony railings at moments like these.

And if you missed that you could still listen to a speech by Mr Horatio Bottomley, the outspoken editor of the magazine *John Bull* – 'The Man Who Foretold the War With Germany' on Monday 30 August at 2.45pm. He was well received and presumably did not harangue his audience with a series of repetitions of 'I told you so'.

The Petty Sessions for the Borough of Ryde gives us a snapshot of life in the Isle of Wight during the war. In April and May absentees from the 4th Battalion the Warwickshire Regiment, one from the Royal Engineers and one from HMS *Pembroke* were found and returned under escort to their units. A deserter from the 2nd Wessex Brigade was charged 5 shillings and a similar reward was given to Frank Ryall, the policeman who apprehended him. Willi Otto Meyer, aged 24, was charged with being an Alien without registration under the Defence of the Realm Act. He could not pay his 5 shilling fine, so

6. Sir Henry Newbolt 1917 *The War Films*

he went to gaol in Winchester for seven days instead. It was not only the Aliens themselves who fell foul of the new government restrictions; anyone failing to report them paid the price too; Eva Williams handed over 5 shillings in July.

Most of the DORA incidents in 1915 and 1916 refer to lack of lights on vehicles. It is obvious that most of the guilty (and the innocent for that matter) regarded this sort of thing as the interference of a 'big brother' state (although it would be another thirty-four years before George Orwell conjured up the picture in *1984*). Presumably, Lieutenant R J Nicolle, as an officer and a gentleman, was able to argue the lack of lights on his bike with some persuasion; the case was withdrawn. In November, Mabel Matthews was not so lucky. The sad 18-year-old had attempted suicide, which was a crime and for which she was hauled before the magistrates. She was committed to Whitecroft, the Island's lunatic asylum, where, by 1915 there was only one resident doctor and a shortage of nurses.

Perhaps, as another Christmas at war loomed, more men than ever wanted to get away from the prospect of serving. Four men, whose unit is not recorded but is probably the Warwickshire regiment, absconded together on 20 December. They were all caught and taken back to barracks under military escort where the army meted out its own glasshouse-style punishment.

The previous August, Charles Hands, a Fleet Street journalist who wrote for the *Daily Mail* and knew Ventnor well, wrote of the town – It was 'no longer polluted by Germans ... but so far the English people have not discovered the Island.' About two-thirds of pre-war visitors to the place, with its palm trees, Isolation Hospital and sub-tropical climate were Germans and Austrians. And Hands was sure that the Germans would be back –

'There is no doubt whatever in Ventnor and Shanklin that one of the aims of German naval policy is the possession of the Isle of Wight and its conversion into a Heligoland fortress ... a Gibraltar of the Channel. The Kaiser, they believe in Ventnor, desires the Island for his own.'

If this is all a little tongue-in-cheek, Hands was more accurate when he says, 'There will never more be a German season on the Undercliff.'

Drunkenness among munitions workers in Cowes became a problem in September. The General commanding the Portsmouth Garrison warned of crews of transport and munitions workers being intoxicated. The Islanders complained vociferously that it was the drafted-in Northerners who were causing these problems, painting their names on chairs and causing trouble if anyone else tried to sit in them. Licensing hours would be cut under Para. 10, Defence of the Realm Acts. Pubs were now open only 12-2.30 and 6-9.

'"Treating" by any one is absolutely forbidden.' When David Lloyd George became Prime Minister later in the war, he said, 'We are fighting Germans, Austrians and Drink and so far as I can see the greatest of these deadly foes is Drink.' The restrictions seemed to have worked. Nationally, the consumption of alcohol had dropped by nearly 50 per cent by the end of the war.

If all this sounds like Orwell's future state, true censorship had still not kicked in. It was not until January 1916 that Vivian Carter, the editor of the magazine *The Bystander* was dismissed for allowing a cartoon of a drunk soldier to appear in print. *The Times* called it 'a gross libel on the Forces of His Majesty'. The *County Press* carried large chunks of a letter written by Sergeant Arthur Odell of the 6th Berkshire Regiment, to his parents in Crocker Street, Newport. The man had been a printer at the newspaper before his enlistment.

'We had our first taste of trench mortars or "sausages" as they are called ... It generally happens like this. You are standing in a trench when suddenly you find the ground moving and before you can move yourself the earth seems as if it has shifted back a foot and then fallen forward with a bump ... then, either under you or in front, it opens and belches out a tremendous burst of flame and smoke and tons of muck ... if you don't pull yourself together and get on what is left of the parapet and open fire you will find a mile of Germans coming at you with fixed bayonets. Oh, we do see life!'

Arthur Odell saw death too, plenty of it, but he made it home.

On 6 November, Arthur Morris, an electrical engineer for the Isle of Wight Railway Company's Locomotive Works in Ryde was accused of 'causing the disaffection of the civil population', a 'very serious offence' which carried a £5 fine or one month in gaol. Ernest Bartlett, a driller in the same works had overheard him say that the Kaiser was the best man in the world. 'What about our king?' Bartlett asked Morris. 'Our king,' Morris said, 'Three cheers for the Fatherland ---- King George!' Minutes earlier, he had said to Bartlett, 'Hello, you ---- Chinaman, have you come to pinch something?' Morris told the court that all this was in jest. He was an Englishman, his parents were English and he had never been out of England. What *was* all the fuss about? The magistrate reminded him there was a war on and fined him five pounds.

Everybody knew there was a war on by September because the McKenna duties kicked in, slapping a huge 33 per cent on imported foreign goods like clocks, cars, musical instruments and – bizarrely – hats. Dachshunds ceased to be popular now; not only were they German but the Germans actually ate them, the more rabid Press contended. German toys like Steiff teddy bears were banned in British shops but wealthier Island families would have been able to buy very realistic home-produced toys that Christmas. An anti-aircraft Maxim Gun, 'beautifully made in solid brass' cost 10/9d.

Boys would always be boys, and some boys' fathers still had the money to indulge them.

'How are the works of His wisdom seen
In the Year of your Lord nineteen-fifteen.'[7]

7. John Drinkwater

Chapter Three

1916

'Oh, wither are you gone, my company?'[8]

Oh! Bright New Year – oh! Glad New Year,
Let all dissensions cease.
Look into the depths of the crystal clear
And give us lasting Peace.'

SO WROTE V H G W Gould in the *Isle of Wight Observer* in January 1916. It all looked rather pessimistic. The papers carried news of casualties. Rifleman Albert Coward of B Company, IW Rifles, a 'sturdily built' boy who had gone through Suvla Bay without a scratch or any sickness, was killed in action. He had been a keen boxer and cross-country runner, a member of the St John's Athletics Club in Ryde and a member of St John's Bible Class. Francis Foot was the tallest man in the Rifles and worked at Pack's store before the war. He died of dysentery and was buried at sea. Bandsman Mowbray suffered from the same condition but he was still alive in the Citadel Hospital, Cairo. Rifleman F Salter was in hospital in Alexandria with peritonitis and P Knight was there too. He had been shot through a lung and the bullet had smashed three ribs, but he was out of danger and had written to his wife. What kind of war was it, the people at home must have wondered, when Rifleman W Quantrill wrote of freezing conditions and four inches of snow and another soldier (unnamed) could die of sunstroke in Aden?

Quartermaster Sergeant WS Russell wrote to his parents who kept the Falcon Inn in Swanmore Road, Ryde. He was on his way late in December to Alexandria and the transport was not marvellous. 'Any old tub suits me,' he wrote, 'as long as it gets me away from the hell of Gallipoli.' Men around him were in agony with frostbite or dying from exposure despite the best attentions of the medics. It never seemed possible to get clothes dry.

The local Press now attacked Conscientious Objectors. The national figures for these men in 1914-18 stood at 16,000. There were 9,000 appeals, half of which resulted in being sent to do work of national importance. 140 were imprisoned for life and fifty for twenty-five years. Seventy of them died in prison, which is such a high proportion that it is likely they were murdered by

---

8. Herbert Reed MC, DSO, *My Company*, Green Howards

fellow inmates. Thirty-five 'conscies' were sentenced to death in courts martial, although in all cases the sentence was commuted.

The list of killed and wounded continued to grow and reference was made to the *Falaba* and the *Lusitania* and the loss of 2000 innocent civilian lives. How could 'conscies' stand by on some theoretical principle when this was the reality of modern war? The authorities took a more sympathetic and enlightened view than the public, who equated pacifism with cowardice. In September when conscription was underway, four brothers from the Brown family of Sandown, faced a Military Tribunal (see below) because they had not registered for exemption. One of them was sent for military service, despite his protestations – and it would be fascinating to know how he coped at the Front. The others were seconded to do work of national importance. The magistrate's intended irony was not lost on the court – 'they [the Browns] were willing to work for 7^1/$_2$d an hour, but not for a shilling a day.'[9]

HJ Woods, a jeweller and outfitter from Sandown was another 'conscie' who objected to war on moral grounds. He had not even liked singing patriotic songs at school, likening it to singing to heathen gods. He refused to supply officers with clothing because it was helping the war effort. So was farming – if he took to the plough it would release others for the Trenches. He was a teetotaller and had recently been receiving threatening letters in the post. He had been a Boy Scout, but because of the movement's military tendencies (they wore uniforms and were raised by a soldier, General Baden Powell) his father had removed him. The Chairman of the Military Tribunal shook his head and brought laughter to the court when he said, 'If you took intoxicants you might be assisting the revenue.' (It was true that a bottle of Scotch which was 3/6d pre-war now cost 4/6d). Woods was given two weeks reprieve before being sent to prison.

Chuckles in magistrates' courts were commonplace, no doubt all part of Islanders' ability to cope with the relentless bad news. William Williams of Spencer Road, Ryde, had no light on his hand cart on 10 January and complained to the magistrate that the policeman who had pulled him over was rude to him. 'Were you polite to him?' the magistrate asked. 'Yes, sir,' Williams replied, 'but he is so deaf he could not hear what I said.'

On 26 February a recruiting advertisement appeared in the Press – 'Single men! Last Days for Voluntary Enlistment at the Drill Hall in Newport. God Save the King.' The decision to bring in conscription was not taken lightly. It smacked of foreignness – the French under Napoleon had had their *levée en masse* – and it was the ultimate in the bullying tactics of the state. Over half of the 8,700,000 men of Britain and the Empire who fought in the Great War were volunteers, but the war was a bottomless pit and now there would be little choice for the able-bodied. The Military Service Bill had been pushed through on 5 January. It

9 The king's shilling was the traditional pay of an enlisted man, dating back to the early nineteenth century. By 1916, the pay was anything between 1/6d to 6s depending on any special duties and separation allowances.

Newport Town Hall was a focus for information during the war. Military Tribunals were held here from 1916 to 1918 to assess exemption claims from military service. Flags flew from the flagpost on Armistice Day 1918 and the streets were packed with revellers. *(Trow)*

applied to single men and childless widowers aged 18 to 40 and this was extended to *all* men by April. In 1918 the upper age limit was extended to 51. There were exemptions, of course, and the men of Isle of Wight qualified more than most because of the large numbers of them involved in agriculture but those exemptions now had to be proved and this was the work of the Military Tribunals. These sprang up in all the major Island towns and even small ones like St Helens, not much bigger than a village.

Magistrates, mayors, vicars and prominent landowners sat in judgement of dozens of cases that came before them each week. Some were genuine – an 18-year-old who was a family's breadwinner left to care for his mother and younger siblings found favour with the court and was allowed to stay. Andrew Thomson of Cowes wanted the call-up for his gardener, A E Sweetenham, to be 'postponed' because he needed his services, presumably for spring planting. The chairman was not impressed. 'Sorry to inconvenience you, Mr Thomson,' he said, 'but the Tribunal is against you. Your man had better join up as soon as he can.'

John Griffiths got away with it. He applied to the Tribunal on behalf of his son Thomas, who assisted in his coal export business in Union Street. This was counted as a reserved occupation and young Thomas never saw the fields of Flanders.

Colonel Howard Brooke asked for a month's postponement on behalf of his chauffeur, A J Newbury and this was granted. Hanry Caws, a butcher of Cowes High Street, had two serving sons already and was granted exemption for his remaining boy as long as the lad continued in the family business. Mrs Baker, a widow, appealed on behalf of her 'conscie' son, not because of his standards, but because he was her only support. She had already written directly to Lord Kitchener who had ignored her – 'This is not justice,' she screamed at the Chairman. 'In Russia, they don't take a widow's son.'

One tragic case that did not come before a Tribunal was that of Arthur Marlow, a Ryde baker with premises in Union Street and Cross Street. With all the irony of the phosgene and mustard gas attacks now commonplace on the Western Front, Marlow gassed himself in his home in May. His suicide note spoke of the strain he was under, having to do the work of three men who had been conscripted. 'I thought I was doing my best,' he wrote, 'Only myself to blame.' Not everyone saw it like that – some blamed the Hun; others the callous high-handedness of Asquith's government.

The Tribunals took a dim view of men who came before them and were clearly trying it on. The well-to-do as we have seen claimed to be absolutely unable to cope without the services of a butler, a chauffeur, a gardener. In virtually every case the Tribunal dismissed the appeal and the lackey was on his way to the Front within days, to become familiar with the itchy, ill-fitting khaki, the mysteries of the .303 Lee Enfield and the 'battle bowlers', the tin hats newly issued which *might* just save lives.

An 'Islander Doing His Bit' wrote to the *County Press* on 8 April –

'On reading the reports of the proceedings of the Island Military Tribunals
I was surprised to see that so many young men have been encouraged by
their employers to get exempted from serving their country. Although so
many men have given up home and everything to fight for the country and
maintain the reputation and good name of the Island, such people as these
are letting it down. Men of the Wight, don't let us down now that we are
getting the upper hand! [sic!] Help your comrades and don't hold back.'

That Easter, the Irish went on the warpath themselves. As early as September 1914 Island papers had been warning about the risk of war with Ireland and now it looked like reality. Frank Lavars, an ex-*Isle of Wight Observer* reporter was in Dublin in April to witness the birth of the poet WB Yeats' 'terrible beauty' first hand. Until the collapse of Russia the following year, Germany was fighting a

A sweetheart badge of the Cyclist Corps, Hampshire Regiment. These were worn by wives and sweethearts of soldiers in the unit. *(Greenham)*

war on two Fronts, having to split her forces East and West. A full scale war with Ireland would put Britain in the same position. Throughout the war a total of 210,000 Irishmen fought for Britain because they were 'John Bull's other island'. The 36th Ulster Division were Protestants from the north and the 10th and 16th were Catholics from the south. It is possible that many volunteered to fight in the belief that independence from Britain would be granted automatically once the war was over. The Easter Rising, romantic and desperate, was confined to Dublin and did not find the dedicated following that its leaders hoped for. Even so, it triggered seven years of violence in the province, known as the Troubles and led to the creation of Eire in 1923.

In the Isle of Wight, as all over Britain, life had to go on. 'Society' weddings still took place, although at Lent people were urged to carry on 'patriotic fasting' – quite how this would help the war effort is not very clear. The papers were full of the long lists of expensive wedding presents given to happy couples by their huge guest lists. In Russia this sort of thing was ammunition which the revolutionaries were storing up against the wealthy whose days were numbered. At the other end of the social scale and here at home, Georgina Mursell, aged 50 and her daughters Minnie, 19 and Elsie, 18 were charged with keeping a disorderly house in Worsley Terrace, Sandown. The word 'bordello' was exotic, upper class and foreign. Perhaps soldiers in France had come across these things in Paris, but it would not do for the Isle of Wight! 'Brothel' was much too bald a word, so 'disorderly house' would have to do and everyone knew what that meant. The police kept a careful watch on the place and noticed soldiers coming and going at all hours of the day and night. Mrs Mursell tried to brazen it out in the magistrates' court. One of the soldiers was Minnie's young man and the others were his friends who had come in to 'warm themselves'. The magistrate did not buy the madame's euphemisms. Georgina was fined £5, Elsie £2 and Minnie, who may actually have had a 'young man', was discharged.

In March and April, a feel-good approach seems to permeate the local Press. Lawrence Dawson of the Sailors and Soldiers Institute in Alexandria felt moved to write of the Isle of Wight Rifles who were passing through on their way to join General Allenby's offensive in the Middle East.

Signalman Fry was one of thousands of soldiers who had himself photographed with the obligatory camel and native handlers in front of the sphinx in Egypt. The regiments posted to Gallipoli came back that way in December 1915. Some stayed in the Middle East while others were sent to the Western Front. *(Matthews)*

'I was shown photographs by the dozen,' Dawson wrote, 'of wives, children and sweethearts – all very proud of their families ... They read the Island papers and know all that happens at home.' And everybody was buoyed up by the extraordinary survival of Rifleman Sid Porter – 'the man the Turks could not kill'. He had been hit by shrapnel only a few days after the landing at Suvla Bay and was left for dead. He was moaning and trying to get up as the Turks reached him so one of them put a bullet in his neck, then bayoneted him. When the burial party arrived, to fling corpses into a common grave on some disputed Gallipoli hillside, Porter was still alive, so he was beaten around the head with a shovel. In the end his attackers gave up and took him prisoner. When he reached the camp he was treated for seventeen different wounds and became the camp barber!

An editorial in April echoes a point made by officers and the Royal Army Medical Corps throughout the war. Lieutenant Charles Carrington of the 1/5th

Battalion Warwickshire Regiment said,

> 'When [the recruits] came to us they were weedy, sallow, skinny frightened children – the refuse of our industrial system – and they were in very poor condition because of wartime food shortages. But after six months of good food, fresh air and physical exercise they changed so much their mothers wouldn't have recognised them.'

Carrington was probably talking about city boys but the rural poverty of the Isle of Wight – which had seen many families try their luck in other parts of the Empire before the war began – produced very similar results. The editorial also pointed out however that with the appalling death rate, there was a greater need than ever to look after the children, because they would be the citizens of Empire of the future.

Looking after the children was not as easy as it had been. The absence of father-figures was a major problem, both because the principal bread-winner had gone (separation allowances from the Front were often late or inadequate) and because of the absence of a strong role model. Mrs Sheaf of Robin Hood Street, Newport, had five children and the eldest was Ronald. He (sometimes) attended Barton School on the edge of the town where the fearsome, yet kindly, headmaster, William 'Skipper' Ouseley, who would be given an MBE for his fund-raising during the war, received a desperate letter from Mrs Sheaf.

> 'Dear Sir,
>
> I am writing to know if you would give my Ronald a good thrashing.' Ronald had done a bunk with money she had given him to get some medicine for her from the chemists; he had spent it on the cinema, sweets and cakes and was gone for eight hours. 'I can't do anything with him,' the bed-ridden Mrs Sheaf complained, longing for the reassurance of her husband's belt on the boy. 'He is always going to the pictures [the Medina Cinema in Newport High Street]. I'm sure I don't know where he gets his money from as his father is away in France so he takes advantage of him being away. I don't think he will be any better until he is put away somewhere.'[10]

It is unlikely that 'Skipper' Ouseley had anywhere to put the boy other than over his knee and whether he actually caned the lad is not recorded. The feral children of the Second World War, the children of the Blitz, are often cited as the most delinquent generation in British history but the same was not true of lads like Ronnie Sheaf and the other 'Boneheads' of Barton School. Most of them went on to become solid citizens trying to cope with the post war world.

Although it barely merits a mention in Island newspapers, the naval battle of Jutland was fought at the end of May. It could have been disastrous, with Vice

10. Quoted in Greening, Brian *History of Barton School 1916-54* privately printed.

Admiral von Scheer's twenty-seven Capital ships against Sir John Jellicoe's thirty-seven. As Winston Churchill wrote later, 'Jellicoe was the only man on either side who could lose the war in an afternoon.' The Germans claimed the tactical victory but it barely made a dent in the British fleet and command of the seas remained with us. Admiral David Beatty took the brunt of German firepower, prompting his famous comment to his Number Two – 'There seems to be something wrong with our bloody ships today.' Many Islanders died that day; there was hardly a town or village left unaffected.

News of heroism came via letters, official despatches and the Island Press every week. In late April Lieutenant RL Flux, a solicitor from Sandown who was serving with the 1/5th Hampshire Howitzer Battery of the Royal Field Artillery was awarded the Military Cross. In temperatures of 115°F he had crawled out over No Man's Land under Turkish fire no fewer than seven times to fix damaged telephone lines. Captain George Hewitt of the 48th Pioneers, Indian Army was awarded the DSO in the same action at Gaza.

There was concern for the present in the form of bread shortages and an article in the *Observer* explained how to make it at home. The Food Controller, Lord Devonport, tried to persuade people to eat less bread. 'Save the Wheat,' said the posters, 'Protect the Fleet,' and boiled rhubarb leaves were suggested as a tasty alternative. Unfortunately, rhubarb leaves contain oxalic acid, known to cause kidney damage and many people became ill.

And there was concern for the future. In an editorial entitled 'The Unspeakable Hun', the writer pondered the post-war world. The unwritten assumption, of course, was that we would win, but this was in the weeks of optimism before the Somme and that would not last. 'Are we,' the editorial asked, 'to forgive and forget? We shall be worse than fools; we shall be madmen if we do.'

Death on the Home Front became reality in May when WT Hollis, whose parents lived in the Strand in Ryde, was killed in the German bombardment of Lowestoft on the East Coast. But it was the celebrity death of Lord Kitchener, Secretary of State for War that caused most consternation when he went down on board the *Hampshire* in June. Today we can see Kitchener in context. He was a meddling busybody who annoyed senior generals and bullied civilian politicians. Along with Winston Churchill, he must carry the lion's share of blame for the failure of Gallipoli because he resolutely refused to let General Ian Hamilton have enough men or ammunition to succeed. He was also a hidebound traditionalist who refused to approve the development of the war-winning tank. Margot Asquith's daughter, Elizabeth Bibesco, famously said of him, 'If he was not a very great man, he was at least a very great poster,' – although this is often attributed to Margot Asquith herself, she never took credit. At the time, however,

Kitchener assumed near sainthood and the obituary report is full of doom and gloom. Alone of the Nationals, the *Daily Mail* blamed the man (rightly) for the shell shortage. Such was the slavish admiration for Kitchener that the paper's sales fell by a million in a month.

Still, local and international businesses cashed in on the war. An arty advertisement for furniture makers Purnells of Ryde read 'How to Gain the V-C' and interspersed with these words were others, so that the whole thing read '**How to gain** ease and comfort at minimum cost, **The** question of today. See and try the **V-C**hair.'

What appears to be an article on the British/Russian alliance is nothing of the sort, as the last paragraph reveals. 'In peace and war De Reszke Cigarettes have proved a real solace, a cigarette that is pleasantly prophetic of the coming trade Entente between two great nations.'

Not to be outdone, a London advertisement for 'home grown' tobacco appeared in Island papers in June. 'Remember the Boys fighting on all fronts and at sea. They want their favourite brands of cigarettes.' And these, Woodbine, Gold Flake, Navy Cut and Three Castles could be sent to loved ones via the Military Forwarding Office in Union Street, Ryde. Cigarettes – known as 'gaspers' to the men in the trenches – feature heavily in cartoons, drawings and

An impressive turnout of the Brooke, Brighstone and Shorwell detachment of the Isle of Wight Volunteers. These men, although the second wave of defence and recruited from those too old or unfit for front line service, seem well armed and equipped. *(Trickett)*

paintings of the period. It was the height of decadence for a woman to smoke in public – there were warnings about female moustaches being caused by the movement of the lips – but for men it was not only acceptable, it was healthy and expected. The *Weekly Despatch*'s 'Smokes for Tommy' campaign led to a quarter of a million pounds being raised in 1916.

In June a new volunteer unit was set up – the 1st Battalion of the Isle of Wight Volunteer Regiment. A Corps had been set up at the very start of hostilities but now that conscription was under way, they came into their own. An inaugural meeting in Ryde Town Hall was not that well attended, but another followed for recruitment purposes at Havenstreet two months later and since details of meetings and training notices were printed thereafter in the local papers each week, it must have been successful. These men were the 'Dad's Army' of their day, men too old or unfit for active service, either with the Regulars or the Territorials. A photograph of the Brooke, Brighstone and Shorwell Detachment shows 53 men and two officers. The captain in command is Aubrey Wickham, who was a county JP and was present at the inaugural meeting. The men's cap badge seems to be the royal coat of arms, which was worn by Other Ranks of all units, Regular and Volunteer, on their tunic buttons. They seem well

The Bible of Wilfred Joliffe. The dedication was written on the first day of the Somme. Many soldiers carried Bibles or books of Psalms in their tunic pockets. *(Greenham)*

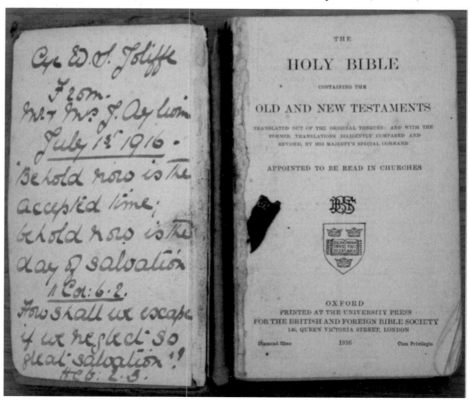

The writing case of Corporal Joliffe of the Hampshire Regiment, complete with pencils, rubber and other memorabilia. Most soldiers used pencils to write with because of the difficulty of using ink in dugouts and trenches. *(Greenham)*

equipped, with .303 rifles and webbing. All are wearing puttees (which men in the Trenches hated putting on) and Captain Wickham sports a pair of leather Stohwasser gaiters popular with officers of the cavalry. Only one man, Phil Jacobs, has no uniform, so he has paraded in bowler and suit. The figure in the centre, Walter Jackman, seems to be in his seventies. These men saw no active service overseas, but took over the duties of the Regulars in guarding military installations and patrolling beaches.

A casualty in July was Captain AC Purnell of the 16th Middlesex Regiment. His commanding officer wrote to his mother, living at St Clair in the Strand, Ryde. Purnell was reported missing and his body found later. His dog tags were given to the Adjutant who sent them home to his family. The man was 35 and one of six brothers at the Front.

The colonel's letter was typical of those that wanted to spare families as much grief as possible – 'He must have died almost at once' was not much comfort, but it often hid an even more ghastly reality. Robert Graves summed up the situation brilliantly in his poem *The Leveller* –

'Yet in his death this cut-throat wild
Groaned "Mother! Mother!" like a child.
While that poor innocent in man's clothes
Died cursing God with brutal oaths.

Old Sergeant Smith, kindest of men,
Wrote out two copies, there and then
Of his accustomed final speech
To cheer the womenfolk of each:-

"He died a hero's death; and we
His comrades of A Company
Deeply regret his death; we shall
All deeply miss so true a pal".'[11]

The following did not appear in Island newspapers, but they are a stark reminder of what war was really all about –

'I curse a sapper [Engineer] beside me. He eyes me vacantly – for he is dead. More and more shells, two of them right in our midst. Shrieks of agony and groans all around me. I am splashed with blood. Surely I am hit, for my head feels as though a battering ram has hit it. But no, I appear not to be, although all about me are bits of men and ghastly mixtures of cloth and blood.'[12]

And perhaps this was what Captain Purnell's commanding officer actually saw when he found the man's body –

'Until the dead are buried they change somewhat in appearance each day. The colour change in Caucasian races is from white to yellow, to yellow-green, to black. If left long enough in the heat the flesh comes to resemble coal-tar, especially where it has been broken or torn and it has quite a visible tarlike iridescence. The dead grow larger each day until they become quite too big for their uniforms, filling these until they seem blown tight enough to burst.'[13]

Early in August Mrs Flux set about organising food parcels for the prisoners, including her son, now a Captain in the 1/5th Hampshire Battery, RFA. She had

11. Robert Graves, Royal Welch Fusiliers.
12. Anthony R Hossack, Queen Victoria's Rifles, quoted in Arthur, Max *The Faces of World War One* p 208
13. Hemingway, Ernest *A Natural History of the Dead*, quoted in Arthur, Max p 97.

Trench art originated in the hands of soldiers serving in France and elsewhere to while away the days and often weeks of boredom. The brass of shell cases was used to fashion vases, inkwells and vesta (match) cases. The Broderick cap of the British Army lent itself well to this sort of work. This example is dated January 1917. *(Trow)*

Trench art made into a vesta (match) case, commemorating the *entente cordiale* between Britain and France. On the back are the initials E.Y. (Essex Yeomanry?) *(Trow)*

received a letter from him saying that the food was quite good but there were no English vegetables and the redoubtable Mrs Flux galvanized her many friends and sympathizers into providing them. A British force sent to protect the Anglo-Persian oil interests had become besieged by the Turks at Kut-el-Amara in December 1915. They clung on desperately with no relief in sight until March 1916 and were then forced to surrender. 720 men of the Hampshires were in Turkish hands – their appalling treatment would not be known until the end of the war – and 72 of them came from the Island.

Trench art, this time in the form of a spoon, etched with a floral decoration and the words 'World War'. On the reverse of the bowl are more flowers and a shield, which may represent a town crest 'somewhere in France'. *(Trow)*

The summer of 1916 was dominated by General Haig's offensive on the Somme which has become a byword for pointless slaughter. Today's revisionist historians have tried to rehabilitate Haig, to claim that his strategy was essentially sound. Tell that to the 19,240 men who died on a single day, 1 July.

On that first day, Captain WB Nevill of the 8th East Surreys used an extraordinary piece of battlefield psychology. Fully aware that his men were about to be cut to pieces, he handed out four footballs and ordered the lads forward, dribbling the balls as they went, as if the enemy Fire trench was an opponent's goal-mouth. He himself was killed but his Division took Montauban and covered themselves in glory. The seven days of bombardment had not destroyed the German trenches. The barbed wire was still intact and the Maxim guns mowed down the Tommies moving at a walking pace across No Man's Land. Those still standing in the next twenty minutes were pounded to oblivion by German artillery and the total killed, wounded, missing and captured stands at 57,470, a day of horror and

Survival in the dash across No Man's Land was largely a matter of luck. Men carried Bibles, prayer books, rosaries and other symbols in a vain attempt to keep themselves safe. This playing card shows the Fumsup character – a baby doll – along with four-leafed clover, wishbones and the swastika. Long before the Nazis adopted the symbol in Germany, it was a Hindu sign of good luck. *(Trow)*

tragedy that the British army had never seen before and hopefully will never see again.

In September Sergeant William Colenutt of the 20th Battalion Canadian Expeditionary Force was killed in France. He had been on leave the previous March at his parents' home in Union Street, Ryde. The Colenutts ran a provisions shop in the town and the blotter (below) is a poignant memory of that. Two little children look out doubtfully into the future, with the single word 'Whither?' printed below them. It is a calendar for 1914 and the answer, for a slightly older generation of boys, was all too obvious two years later.

William Colenutt was one of a number of Islanders who had emigrated to various parts of the Empire before the war to start a new life. Jobs were hard to come by in those pre-war days and cheap passage was arranged for young men who wanted to try their luck elsewhere. Colenutt had gone to Canada but the call to arms in August 1914 meant that some men returned home to enlist in the British army or were shipped to the war zone with their Canadian outfit. Canadian troops at the Somme in June were told that they would be going forward to mop up German survivors and make for the Rhine. That never happened.

Another Islander who emigrated was Bertram Snellgrove. He was one of 20 per cent of the British-born who served with the Australian Imperial Force. He

The Fumsup doll carried by many men in their inside tunic pockets, was tiny (this example is 1¼ inches long). It has a body of brass, with articulated arms and a nut for a head. Rather like the rosary or Greek 'worry' beads, men were encouraged to stroke the head for good luck. *(Trow)*

The Colenutt Blotter, calendar for 1914.

lived in Roma, near Sydney and ran the Federal Bakery there. A cutting from *The Western Star*, dated August 1915 reads –

'Mr B A Snellgrove begs to inform the public that he has joined the colours and that he has secured the services of a first class baker. The business will be carried on as usual by his partner, Mr W Knowles. Mr Snellgrove thanks his numerous customers for their support in the past and hopes for a continuance of

The 'Death Penny' sent to the family of Private Bertram Snellgrove in Australia. These solid brass plaques, with the deceased's name on the cartouche, were posted in dark grey envelopes and sent with an illuminated scroll. *(Downer)*

same during his absence.'

In the same paper, the editorial said,

'Among the recent volunteers is Mr Snellgrove ... of the Federal Bakery. Although Mr Snellgrove has found his country's call irresistible, he is not relinquishing his business and hopes to come safely back to Roma when the war is over ...'

He did not. Private 3539 Bertram Alfred Snellgrove of the 26th Battalion Australian Imperial Force was killed on 29 July 1916.

His name appears on a memorial in Roma erected in 1938 and a tree was planted in his honour – there was one

Private Bertram Snellgrove ran a bakery business in Roma, near Sydney Australia and was killed in France, one of many 'sons of the Empire' who gave their lives. *(Downer)*

The official recognition of a hero. The for commemorative scroll sent to the family of Bert Snellgrove of the Australian Imperial Forces, one of many ex-Islanders who went out to the colonies for a better life. *(Downer)*

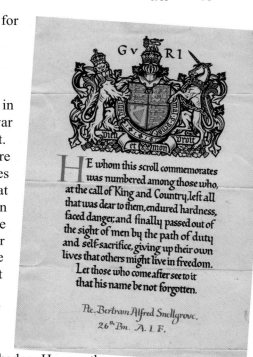

G v R I

HE whom this scroll commemorates was numbered among those who, at the call of King and Country, left all that was dear to them, endured hardness, faced danger, and finally passed out of the sight of men by the path of duty and self-sacrifice, giving up their own lives that others might live in freedom.
Let those who come after see to it that his name be not forgotten.

Pte. Bertram Alfred Snellgrove,
26th Bn. A.I.F.

each of the ninety Roma men who died – in the early 1920s. He is also listed on the war memorial in St Thomas's Square, Newport.

Thousands of men died overseas and were buried in the Belgian and French cemeteries that are poignant reminders of a war that need never have been fought. Others, blown to pieces by shells, have no grave at all. One of these, George Kingswell, was another member of the Australian Imperial Force who died on the same day as Snellgrove at Pozières.

He was 27 and the photograph, probably a studio portrait made in Belgium to send home to his family, shows a proud Aussie with the famous slouch hat and sun-burst badge. He was the son of Edwin and Ann Kingswell of 2, Landguard Villas, Shanklin (a house which no longer stands). All the Kingswell men served. Fred, George's brother, was in the Army Medical Corps – the Red Cross armlet was usually respected by all combatants. Ted (Edwin junior) was a stoker on HMS *Canopus*. These two came home.

It is unusual to find the actual grave of a Tommy here at home. Lance-Sergeant Rowland Brown, whose parents owned Guildford

George Henry Kingswell, No. 3168, of the 28th Battalion, the Australia Imperial Forces who was killed at Pozières in July 1916, aged 27. The famous slouch hat with the sunburst badge was *the* hallmark of the Australians, although Kingswell was an Islander who had left to find his fortune before the war. *(Yates)*

Fred Kingswell, of the Royal Army Medical Corps, survived the war and went on to run the Plough and Barleycorn Inn in Shanklin. Medical orderlies, despite their Red Cross armbands, were unarmed and took huge risks tending wounded men under fire. *(Yates)*

'Some corner of a foreign field' – the Australian war memorial commemorating the dead, including George Kingswell, who fell at Pozières in France. *(Yates)*

Fred Kingswell in the sheepskin issued to troops in the freezing winter trenches. Despite keeping men warm these skins became very heavy and uncomfortable when wet. *(Yates)*

Farm near Havenstreet, was wounded near Beaumont-Hamel and brought home, his leg shattered by a shell. An infection set in and he died in September. His coffin was carried to its place in St Peter's Church, Havenstreet by six sergeants of the Warwickshire Regiment and a firing party of the regiment from Parkhurst barracks aimed their .303s to the sky in a final salute to a brave man. The vicar, AC Roberts, paid tribute and although there is no record of it, it is likely that the whole village turned out to watch a soldier's passing.

In that month of September, the shipbuilders JS White of Cowes went into aircraft production. They built over two hundred aircraft, mostly seaplanes for the Royal Navy. Two Island brothers, test-flying a fighter, crashed into a field at Cockleton Lane,

IN EVER LOVING MEMORY OF
ROWLAND JAMES BROWN,
LCE. SERGT. 14TH HANTS REGT.
SECOND SON OF

R. I. P.

Unusually, this memorial in Havenstreet is actually the grave of the soldier it commemorates. He was invalided home, died of his wounds and was given a regimental funeral. *(Trow)*

Northwood. The inquest could not decide on why the plane had come down. The pilots (unnamed) were competent and the machine not faulty. The verdict was accidental death. 'The jury,' said the *County Press*, 'wished to express their deepest sympathy with the bereaved parents of these two young men, who met their deaths in defence of their country just as much as if they had died facing the foe.'

As if in defiance of the grim reality of the Somme, local editorials for October are full of upbeat drum-beating. They are all about breaks-through and turning points, echoing the propaganda that Asquith's government was churning out and to which the high command of every country clung. It may be that Haig's full frontal tactics were ultimately to grind the enemy down, but at what cost? There were calls for Asquith's resignation.

In the Island, every care was taken to stay alert. Mrs Mary Lusada, the wife of a London solicitor, took a walk along the headland at Totland Bay. She was an amateur artist and her imagination was caught by Hurst Castle across the Solent from her. She began to sketch what she saw. Then DORA intervened. Mrs Lusada found herself in court because she was drawing a military installation which could, presumably, have fallen into enemy hands. Despite her (not unreasonable) protest that she had no idea that she was breaking the law, she was fined £1 and her artwork was destroyed.

By November there were large numbers of convalescent troops on the Island. The hospitals were full, even King Edward's for Officers at Osborne House and a number of institutions were made available for the men as reading rooms and billiard halls. The Longford Institute in Havenstreet fulfilled this role, as did the Welby Institute and the Town Hall in Ryde.

Holmdale House in Havenstreet was built as the Longford Institute and during the Great War was a convalescent home for soldiers. Concerts were put on here and the building still had its stage in the 1980s. *(Trow)*

Sir Charles Seeley pushed the Isle of Wight for yet more volunteers – after all, Sir John French, the former commander-in-chief of the BEF had said in a recent speech in Birmingham that invasion could not entirely be ruled out.

Food costs were rising alarmingly as yet another war Christmas loomed. Eggs which had been 4d each were now 6d, although as in the Second World War, country folk had greater access to produce than those in the towns so the Island was probably better off in this respect than some mainland industrial areas. All over the Island, allotments sprang up to supplement the increasingly meagre rations available in towns. In Barton School, 'Skipper' Ouseley had his children growing strawberries the following summer for jam for the troops. This was just as well. One of the most famous cartoons drawn by Captain Bruce Bairnsfather of the Warwickshire Regiment, as early as September 1915 showed his ubiquitous 'Old Bill' soldier grumbling about the monotony of the plum and apple jam provided by the government. 'When the 'ell,' Bill wonders, 'is it going to be strawberry?' Bairnsfather had been stationed at Parkhurst Barracks in 1915 and one of his Old Bill originals had been auctioned off as a fund raiser.

Ominously, the local papers reminded everyone that the Food Controller had very wide powers; most of the public had no idea that such an individual existed. The soaring cost of fuel led to a strike at J S White's and brought nearly 6,000 men and women out onto the streets. These people were highly skilled in ship and aircraft production and the country could not afford to have their lathes idle. The Controller of Fuel stepped in (nobody knew about him either!) and the price was fixed at 10/- a ton.

But it was Christmas and the advertisements pretended that it was almost business as usual. 'What shall I send him?' a pretty war wife asks herself. The answer, of course, was any of the range provided by the British-American Tobacco Company and a free Christmas card was enclosed with each parcel. The cinema in Ryde was showing *Salambo* over the Christmas period (what today we would call a sword and sandal epic) and tickets were available from Teague's music warehouse in Union Street.

Potentially dubious people were still being brought before the courts, for taking illicit pictures. There is no report of what this particular photograph showed but the guilty party was Lillian Mallard of Newport. She was fined the usual £1 but the magistrate grimly reminded her that if she had used her box Brownie for these purposes in Germany she would have been shot. And even more dubious people were profiting from the war by the end of the year. There were now so many street collections for various worthy causes that national legislation ought to be brought in, said the *County Press*, to weed out the bogus who were pocketing the funds themselves.

The Prime Minister, Herbert Asquith, resigned in December and was replaced by the 'Welsh wizard' David Lloyd George. The Welshman had been Minister of Munitions since May and had worked wonders in the production of shells and new weapons like the Stokes light mortar and the tank. He had used DORA with brilliant efficiency, taking control of railways, factories and mines to coordinate the war effort. Now that he was at Number 10, surely things would improve?

But the *Observer*'s Christmas message was as stark and grim as ever – 'Martyred Belgium, Stricken Serbia, Ravaged Roumania ... There will be thousands of vacant places this Christmastide because of loved ones lost or away with the Colours.' And people could not even drink to forget. W B Mew, Langton & Co, Wine and Spirit Merchants reminded the public that there were restrictions on beer, wine and spirits by Order of the Board of Control. With extreme penalties for breaking these orders, spiralling to a fine of £100 or six months hard labour, it was probably best to stay sober. Lloyd George would have approved.

Chapter Four

1917

'Life, to be sure, is nothing much to lose;
But young men think it is, and we were young.'[14]

FROM TIME TO time, Island newspapers voiced concerns over morality. There was no evidence, magistrates said, that unmarried pregnancies were on the increase ('unlike elsewhere' they added, rather smugly) but at the same time with large numbers of troops in the Island, every care had to be taken. In the August of 1915 the Chairman of the Local Board of Health said that a lot had been written about war babies, but 'he was very pleased to say that they were not suffering from that epidemic in the Island'. There had been sixteen illegitimate births in the previous quarter, as opposed to the usual twelve. 'When you consider,' he said, 'the thousands of military men stationed here during the last year, it is very satisfactory.'

The County Council placed an announcement in January concerning Venereal Disease – 'Although these diseases occur as a result of immoral conduct, they may be spread in other ways.' The public, if not the medical men, accepted wholesale stories of less-than-spotless toilet seats. The Royal Isle of Wight Hospital at Ryde offered free treatment, under conditions of the utmost secrecy. There was no need for a GP or hospital referral and every patient had a number, rather than a name. Rail fare would be provided for the poor. At the other end of the social scale, Lieutenant Colonel Godfrey Collins wrote to the *County Press* to say that in Mesopotamia (an area which today includes part of Turkey, Iraq, Syria and Iran) his men had not seen a woman for nine months. But then, they had not seen a tree or a stone either! The whole question of sex in the Great War is shrouded in secrecy. I have not come across a single letter between a serviceman and his wife/sweetheart so the nature of relationships is rather vague. The various cartoonists of the period used pretty girls in every situation. The women at home are always portrayed as beautiful and young; the nurses in the base hospitals were angels. The German-American artist Raphael Kirchner produced colour plates of lovely girls that were acceptable 'soft porn' by the standards of the time. These were pinned up in dugouts wherever soldiers gathered and in November 1915 the *Sketch*, which published them, printed a poem that captures the mood perfectly –

'When I turned about in the small dug-out.

14. A E Houseman, *Here Dead We Lie.*

My glance on the picture tarried;
So I hied me away from the fair display,
Remembering I was married.'

Some marriages must have gone to the wall during or as a result of the war, although divorce was expensive and not approved of by any social class. In their rest periods behind the lines, the men had access to French and Belgian girls as well as brothels to which the authorities turned blind eyes.

At home, war bonuses went to the gravediggers at Ryde cemetery. They received 2s extra a week. All in all, it was a miserable time. There was a fire at Sivier's Hotel in Ryde and the convalescent soldiers staying there had to go somewhere else. Private William Wining of the Warwickshire Regiment was found hanging in a barn at Westmont, the huge house in Queen's Road that would eventually become Ryde School. He was 26 and had been a groom at the house, owned but rented out by a branch of the Player family, before the war. His family and comrades could not account for his suicide. He was a cheerful man, left no note and seemed to relish the idea of overseas service. Perhaps all that was merely the outward show.

In February, many units left for France, crowding along the pier at Ryde to catch the steamer to Portsmouth. The 'Tank' cafe in Monkton Street, opened by the late Miss Macqueen the previous November, was still open for business as usual however.

The courts and the police were less than sympathetic to people who came to their notice. Reginald Wells, a potato grower from Cridmore was brought before the magistrate on charges of falsifying his age to avoid military service. Ironically, as a food producer, he was exempt anyway. He was fined £10 and sent to the military. Mary Bennett of Down End stole a bike. She was about to start work in a munitions factory in Cowes but her little girl had recently died and her husband had been away for nearly four years. The magistrates put her in prison for one month. Rose Lloyd, from Cowes, missed her husband too and tried to drown herself early in March. Superintendent Galloway, giving evidence in court, said that 'in all his experience he had never before known a woman who intended suicide enter the water without taking her hat off.' She was put on probation.

The recruitment drive continued despite conscription and the weekly ritual of the Military Tribunals. 'No man,' ran the government's advertisement, 'can shirk these responsibilities with a clear conscience' and an official letter was sent to all newspapers in the country – 'To Every Patriotic Citizen from 18 to 61 Years of Age'. The minimum wage (although the term was not used) was fixed at 25 shillings a week. The letter was signed by Neville Chamberlain, who would find himself in the hot seat at 10 Downing Street twenty-two years later when another world war broke out. 'Doing one's bit' had now extended to six days a week for nearly everyone and farmers and labourers found themselves working on Sundays too. There seems to have been little protest from Sabbatarians, possibly because everyone saw the need to pull together.

For those with loved ones at the Front, what better way to keep 'your boy' cheerful, asked the newspapers. Send him the latest copy of *Tit-Bits* – 'the cheeriest and best paper. Keep him Merry and Bright'. Brighter still were the tales of heroism that trickled past the censor – no doubt for positive propaganda reasons. Lieutenant Butler of the Hampshire Regiment sent a letter to Mrs Parsons of Victoria Rd, Newport about the bravery of her son, Rifleman Ernest Parsons. He had found a wounded officer of his unit and had carried the man and his equipment for over a mile under fire to the safety of his lines – 'I'll get you back all right, sir; don't you bother.'

Brightness continued to be a problem as the inhabitants of coastal towns continued to ignore DORA regulations about the blackout. In May, a Ventnor man appeared before magistrates accused of using a 'Zeppelin candlestick' in his bedroom window after dark. When the magistrate asked the arresting officer what a Zeppelin candlestick was, he admitted he did not know, but he knew it was bright and could be seen for miles out to sea.

There are new seats in St Thomas' Square, Ryde, today. They have replaced the original ones put up in April 1917 for use by wounded soldiers, who called them 'Junkers' Rests'. There was the usual dichotomy between the world of advertising and harsh economic reality. The World's

Another member of the Gilbert family in camp. The Sam Browne belt was ubiquitous for officers but this picture shows the Glengarry cap, cut away tunic, sporran and kilt of the Highland Regiments. Webbing puttees are wrapped around the socks and the ankle boots have iron studs on the soles. *(Boxall)*

Stores at 32, High Street, Ryde, claimed that England was still the cheapest country to live in. Excellent pure butter was only 1/8d a pound. How was it then, that down the road at 71 Union Street, in the same town and the same month, gentlemen's outfitter Arthur Bevis had to declare bankruptcy? It was the old story – in emergency situations the demand for food does not change; treating oneself to a new pair of plus fours was a different matter.

April was the month in which the first air casualty news reached the Island papers. The Royal Flying Corps was not yet the Royal Air Force and the first pilots, buffeted through the clouds in fragile aircraft, were drawn from the cavalry and infantry. Unlike their counterparts in the German and French air forces, British flyers carried no parachutes which were considered too bulky in the cramped canopies of fighter planes. Lieutenant Kenneth Mackenzie whose parents lived in Lansdowne House, John Street, Ryde, was shot down over the German lines in France on Easter Sunday, quite possibly while his parents were at church. He had been attached to the Seaforth Highlanders.

The news from France seemed to go from bad to worse, although most of it did not reach local or even national newspapers because of censorship. Some men had always kept the horrors of war from their families.

Signalman E Fry of the 23rd Division's Signal Company only sent brief postcards home with cheery news about the weather and idyllic pictures of

Every man his own first aider. This sling from Signalman Fry's personal belongings shows accurate drawings of how to bandage and apply tourniquets in the field. These had been issued in the Boer War too. *(Matthews)*

E B Fry's 23rd Signals Company, showing the men with their bandoliers over their shoulders. The motor bikes were used extensively in the Great War as a fast means of communication. *(Matthews)*

tourist France in happier days. The French army having been pummelled at the huge fortress of Verdun in 1916, a massive counter-attack failed in the Champagne region and mutiny broke out. Haig was gearing up for his offensive which would become known as Passchendaele. 250,000 British troops would become casualties to gain four miles of mud.

Things were going better in Palestine, but not, of course, without casualties. Archie Marlow, the son of the overworked baker who had killed himself the previous year, was with the Isle of Wight Rifles when he too died on 19 April. He had been a stalwart member of Ryde Rowing Club and of the Conservative Party whose local offices were in Lind Street. In the *Observer* issue of 19 May, no less than 24 casualties were reported and the War Office asked, rather optimistically, for men up to 50 to volunteer. A letter to the editor asked, sensibly, what possible use middle-aged men would be in a young man's war. They had never

A formal studio portrait of Signalman Fry. He went on to be awarded the MBE in the Second World War. *(Matthews)*

taken military orders in their lives and would probably be more of a hindrance than a help in the circumstances.

Absentees, absconders and deserters continued to be a problem. Ernest Willstead, 20 and Robert Hopejoy, 23, had done a runner from the Royal Field Artillery at Borden Camp in Hampshire and had made their way (unwisely) back home. Likewise, John McFarlane had absented himself from the 14th Battalion the Australian Imperial Force as had George Heskett from the Duke of Cornwall's Light Infantry. They were all handed over to the military.

Aliens Registration Acts continued to be ignored by some people, including Bernard CM de Lisle who sounds very exotic. The Marquise de Saint Gré sounded grander still and she was released, as it is phrased today, on her own recognizance in April. That may have been a generosity too far by Island magistrates; the police discovered that Saint Gré was an alias, but there seems to have been no follow up to this. Whoever she really was, the French lady may have satisfied the courts that she was not a risk to the safety of the nation.

By June concern was being expressed on the situation in Russia and Island papers from 1917 onwards increasingly raided the National Press for news and even editorial slant. The 'Unspeakable Hun' and 'Beastly Boche' rhetoric of the opening months of the war is noticeably less now, although the atrocity of German troops crucifying captured Tommies lingered on in the public mind for years after the Armistice. And it was not true. In March (February in the Old Russian calendar) in the face of continued military defeats, Tsar Nicholas II had been overthrown and placed under house arrest. A provisional middle class government under Prince Lvov took over but its leading light was Alexander Kerensky, the War Minister. The new government had pledged to carry on the war but Kerensky's June offensive failed and thousands of Russian soldiers streamed away from the Front never to fight again or to lend their support to the future Bolshevik government of Lenin.

That was the month that the *Isle of Wight Observer* began a rather tongue-in-cheek column called *On Dit*, claiming that 'the mighty explosion which took place on the Western Front at 3am on Thursday morning [the beginning of the Messines bombardment] was heard by some people in Ryde – perhaps.' Sunday school treats for the kiddies had now stopped because of war shortages and Frank Dore, of John Street, Newport, came the old soldier (literally) when he appeared before magistrates for begging with a barrel organ. Nearly blind, he claimed to have been discharged from the army, which was true. The only problem was that all this had happened 17 years earlier!

The position of the church, in this war as in all wars, was anomalous. The Christian ethic of loving thy neighbour as thyself and turning the other cheek sounded a little hollow in the mud of Flanders, but of course there were those who took comfort from the familiar words of the Sunday service. Hymns like 'Eternal

Father, Strong to Save' and 'Onward Christian Soldiers' were hugely popular in Island churches and chapels and various religious groups did excellent work raising funds for the troops. The vicar of All Saints' Church, Ryde, put his money where his mouth was however on 10 July – he joined the army as a padre.

The first example of idiocy on Ryde Pier was recorded on 16 June. The pier was (and remains) the gateway to the Island for many and two policemen were on duty at the Pierhead checking on the nationality of every arrival and the purpose of their visit. Rather like customs officials at modern airports, these men had no sense of humour at all. So when Private Stanley Lawson of the Motor Troop of the Army Service Corps (often called, rather contemptuously, Ally Sloper's Cavalry) said he was a German, no one (except Lawson) laughed. He was charged with giving false information under the Aliens Order at Cowes. He stood in the dock wearing the khaki he had worn on the pier, complete with ASC cap badge and explained that, in those circumstances, he assumed the policemen would realize he was joking. The magistrate was unamused too; he fined Lawson 5/-. The same policemen had sent back Belgians who appeared in uniform, clearly unable to tell one foreigner (even a member of the Army Service Corps) from another.

The 'flog 'em' brigade were staunchly behind the magistrates. Serious crime all but disappeared from the Island during the war years but petty crimes continued, especially those carried out by juveniles the local papers called 'Bad Boys'. Riding bicycles on pavements was one sign that all sense of civilization had gone; so was 'stealing two lettuce' and 'obtaining cakes by false pretences'. On 29 September an article demanded the birch for tearaway children – 'The trouble arose through a lack of parental control owing to the absence of fathers on service – it would pass away with the war' but in the meantime 'the recommendation simply aimed at punishing indecent conduct on the part of young blackguards, who richly deserve a thrashing which they will never forget.'

Still, as the anniversary of the beginning of the war neared, there was a resolve to carry on as usual – 'facing the fourth year undismayed'. A public meeting was held at the town halls throughout the Island and a number of regiments, Regular and Territorial, were represented. In each one a resolution was officially passed to continue 'a righteous war'. Over the years the righteousness of 1914-18 has been seriously challenged. There are post-revisionist historians today who say that this is correct, that the Kaiser was bent on European domination in 1914 as Hitler would be in 1939. This ignores completely the culpability of all the other countries (including Britain) who were signatories to various military alliances and the fact that the Kaiser tried in the first week of August 1914 to call off mobilization.

The 'Tank' had closed in Ryde earlier in the year but a new canteen for soldiers had been opened by Miss Greenup at Mount House School in George

Street. Soldiers were welcome between 6.30 and 9.30pm. A celebrity arrived in Ryde in September when Lord French inspected the Worcestershire Regiment drawn up in the gardens of Westmont. Islanders flocked in their hundreds to cheer and to wave flags. The mood of the autumn was a strange combination of superstitious dread and muted optimism. There was talk that Lord Kitchener, who had gone down on the *Hampshire* as the most high-profile of the war's casualties, was still alive. An editorial in the *Observer* demanded that the government quash the rumours at once. 'We hear a great deal,' wrote the paper's editor, 'about a world league of nations which is to act the part of international policeman ...'

The League, which would be set up during 1919 during the protracted peace negotiations, had, like its successor, the United Nations, a built-in weakness. Especially after a bloodbath like 1914-18, no country seriously wanted to go to war again to win the peace and countries squabbled between themselves within the League's chamber, negating the whole *raison d'être* of the League's existence. In September 1917 no doubt it sounded like a good idea. In what was an all-too-typical week, the *County Press* issued its casualty list. JW Raeburn of the Canadian Force, from Newport; A Ricks of the Royal West Kent Regiment; A Rogers of the Hampshires, from Sandown and G H Taylor, a driver with the Royal Engineers were all reported killed. The next batch were those earlier believed to be missing, now known to be dead, which can have come as no surprise to their grieving families – Lieutenant E Clayton, with the Royal Flying Corps from Ventnor; Private L Kinshott, the Hampshires, from Ryde and Lance-Corporal G Woodford of the Duke of Cornwall's Light Infantry from Newport. Five men – H Carter, A Froud, E Harwood, F Henstridge and W Peck had all died of wounds and five more – W Gladdis, F Draper, A Brett, F Diffey and A Warren – had died as Prisoners of War.

Mrs W H Grace of Alverstone, Whippingham, placed a personal advertisement asking for details of her missing son, Lieutenant CJ Tolman, 22 Squadron RFC. No one had heard from him since 27 September.

The following week carried more details on these men. William Gladdis of the Royal Berkshires had died in hospital at Le Cateau with a gunshot wound that had ruptured a lung. Gunner Herbert Carter of the Siege Battery, Royal Garrison Artillery, came from Arctic Road in Cowes and his late father had been an army man too. He had served for eight years, six of them in the safety of India. He had only been in France for eleven weeks when a shell shattered his chest. 'Another promising young townsman has made the supreme sacrifice on the Western Front.' This was Archie Froud, the youngest son of Councillor J Froud of Park Road in Ryde. The boy had been hit by shrapnel in the chest and right leg but what killed him were the after-effects of gas 'and he suddenly succumbed'. Depending on the type used, gas caused blindness, deafness, vomiting and death. A nurse on the Western Front described such victims – 'The poor things – burnt and blistered all over with great mustard-coloured suppurating blisters, with blind eyes, all sticky and stuck together and always fighting for breath, with voices a mere whisper, saying their throats are closing and they know they will choke.'

George Woodford was 26, the eldest of four 'fine soldier sons' who had been missing for weeks. Not in the original casualty list, Private C Hutchings of the Wiltshire Regiment was 19. His parents lived at 98, Hunnyhill in Newport and he had been wounded in both legs, the side and right arm by shell fire. He had been temporarily buried in a dug-out when the roof collapsed on him. Both his legs had been amputated above the knee.

Alfred Ricks of St Aubyns, Staplers, Newport, was the proprietor of a 'well known restaurant' in Lower High Street in the town. William Peck, whose father ran the Britannia pub in Hunnyhill had joined up at the start of the war. He served on the Western Front, in Salonika and in Palestine where he died. 'It was in the dash on Nazareth that he was fatally wounded. His officer spoke highly of this promising young soldier.' It must have struck Peck's parents how ironic it was that their third son should lose his life in the very village where the son of God lived out much of his own short life.

In November – and for the first time – the Island's newspapers carried a new worry. When the war was finally over, how could the men who fought return to a normal life? Laying aside the horrors they had experienced – almost no-one recognized the traumas of the battlefield then – women had in many cases usurped their jobs. They worked in munitions factories, drove the teams at the plough and worked on buses and trams. Vitally important to the war effort though their work was, this was something that might come to bite men in the backside before too long. Men were given home leave to 'Blighty' every fourteen months and these times were emotional roller-coasters. The bliss of homecoming was short-lived if only because men knew this could not last. One man famously refused to go on leave – 'I said Goodbye, sir, when we left home. I couldn't stand to do it again.' Some men felt guilty. They were spending seven days with their loved ones, but their loved ones could not understand their experiences or sympathize genuinely with what their men-folk had been through. Soldiers realised that their real families were the lads at the front who knew 'the Hell where youth and laughter go'. Still others were furious at the slackers and shirkers hiding behind reserved occupations and the whingeing of people complaining about rationing and the cost of living. Whatever the cost, it was cheaper than dying.

But it was two international developments that gave thinking Islanders pause for thought as the end of 1917 neared. The first concerned Russia and the editor of the *Observer* was in doubt about the gravity of the situation – 'Her deplorable failure is the tragic calamity of 1917.' Kerensky's government fell in November. Vladimir Lenin had been allowed back from exile by the Germans in a sealed train. Winston Churchill likened his arrival to a plague bacillus, not just because he brought with him the evils of Bolshevism but because it was his avowed intention to end the war with Germany. Seizing Petrograd, Moscow and Kiev in a wave of violence, Lenin's Bolsheviks promised the Russian people 'peace, bread and land'. The last two never truly materialised, and the first was illusory for nearly five years, but it meant that the Germans no longer faced their dreaded war on two fronts and could turn their full attention to the west. One million men were released to tackle the British and French.

The other development was the arrival of the Americans, though whether it actually made up for the collapse of Russia is debatable. When the *Lusitania* was sunk by German torpedoes in May 1915, there were 128 Americans on board. We know now that the ship carried arms and ammunition but at the time the British and American public saw this as an unprovoked attack on women and children. Continued attacks on American merchant ships by U boats led to the President, Woodrow Wilson, declaring war on Germany in April 1917. Most Britons saw this as a shameful delay. In one celebrated cartoon in July 1915, Thomas Maybank drew Uncle Sam and the Kaiser for *The Bystander*. Sam is saying, 'If you don't darned well stop this submarine business and cease your murderous attacks on American citizens, we'll – er – er, we'll – hum – well – we'll jolly well send you another firm Note.'[15] In that month alone 430 ships were lost and Britain had less than six weeks corn supply left at that stage. The actual military support of the United States came with agonising slowness. Congress passed a Selective Service Act in May and in June the 1st US Infantry Division arrived in France. The 'doughboys' were inexperienced. They had never faced a modern European army but the propaganda boost to morale was huge and potential numbers incalculable.

In December, the editor of the *Isle of Wight Observer* wrote, 'Looking back on the year 1917 one is moved to a feeling of sympathy with the young people who will be wrestling with history lessons in the next few decades. Every year seems more crowded than the last.'

Seventy-four Islanders had become the 'fallen heroes' of 1917. The total number of wounded is not recorded.

14. Quoted in Gosling, Lucinda, *Brushes and Bayonets* p 136.

Chapter Five

1918

'It seemed that out of battle I escaped ...'[16]

BY THE JANUARY of 1918 the full extent of the Russian situation was commented on by the editor of the *Isle of Wight Observer*. It would be years before the 'iron curtain' of Communism would slam down in front of the Eastern bloc so information, albeit garbled, was coming through from Russia. Leon Trotsky, Commissar of the Red Army, was in protracted negotiations with the Germans right through to March when the Treaty of Brest-Litovsk was ratified. Known as the 'robber peace' it took vast swathes of territory from Russia, a third of her population and farming land, two thirds of her coalmines and half her heavy industry. But it was a buyer's market – if the new USSR was to survive at all, it had to stop fighting Germany. There is an unusually 'political' letter sent by Beryl Flux's uncle to his mother in March. The weather was awful and the German Spring Offensive seemed to have been postponed (and he could not, of course, tell his family where he was) but he had heard that the 'Japs are to assist in Russia so that should help considerably.' It didn't.

In the Isle of Wight meat shortages continued and half a page of the *County Press* was filled with a case in which the maximum price of butter had been exceeded – it was a seller's market here of course. From now on all Island papers are littered with references to the Food Control Committee and to the importing of bacon and ham. Sprats were four times pre-war prices. There was a need to change pig-feed too. Potatoes, maize, barley and peas were now desperately needed for human consumption. Pigs would have to make do with grass, acorns, silage, bran, sharps, dried yeast and waste food products. Had no one told the animals there was a war on?

Accidents were on the increase in the long dark nights because of the removal of street lamps. 'Removal' is too strong a word and that was precisely the point. The lamp *posts* remained in place and a number of people walked into them. *On Dit* suggested they be replaced with rubber ones!

News of the war was referred to, a little coyly perhaps, in the *Observer* as 'Personal War Items' and as 1918 wore on and the military situation improved, more detail was provided about wounds and personnel than previously. Gunner Frank Bridle was wounded in the face, arm and hand and was in hospital in St

---

16. 2nd Lieutenant Wilfred Owen MC, Manchester Regt, killed in action 4 November 1918.

Albans. Bombardier C Williamson of Adgestone was wounded in the shoulder and was in hospital in Leith. Rifleman Downer of the 1/8th Hampshires had dysentery in an Egyptian hospital. Private Arthur Eldridge, also of the Hampshires, was killed at the age of 20. His family lived at 19 Brunswick Street, Ryde.

Amidst the slaughter that was still going on with little sign of a breakthrough, it is a little incongruous, perhaps, to see a London advertisement for Morgan and Scott's Portable Organs. They 'are always handy at the Front or at home for Munition Workers'.

If anything the food shortages got worse in February. There was a punch-up in a margarine queue in Ryde among long-suffering women who had become used to this sort of thing. Island butchers buying their meat in Southampton complained that before the war they usually bought 35 bullocks and 200 sheep. That February they came away with 5 bullocks and 3 sheep. A butcher in Ryde put up a notice in his shop window – 'No use knocking or ringing side bell. Unable to do the impossible.'

There was good news and bad news about the military. A row broke out between Quartermaster Sergeant Michael Carroll and Company Quartermaster Sergeant Henry Shead at the Golden Hill Fort garrison in Freshwater. Shead had been carrying on with Carroll's wife while the latter was in France and the resulting altercation led to Shead shooting Carroll dead with a German pistol he had brought back as a souvenir from the Trenches. The case was referred to Winchester Crown Court. On the other hand, Sergeant F Combes of the South Wales Borderers was given a medal and a watch by the German authorities for saving a little girl from drowning. No details are given but Combes was clearly a Prisoner of War somewhere in Germany. He had been with the BEF – the 'contemptible little army' – since the beginning and had been wounded and captured at Ypres at the end of October 1914.

By the middle of the month a National Kitchen was to be set up at Seaview. This was a country-wide, government-sponsored initiative brought about by the food shortage which in turn was the result of the U-boat menace. The idea did not apply to wartime only, of course – soup kitchens had been set up by charities and volunteers for years in times of particular hardship or slum areas where poverty was the norm.

The figure for dead, wounded and missing is included in the *Observer*'s pages – 254 killed in action and a further 470 wounded or unaccounted for. Twelve Islanders had died in February to date and their names are listed. One of them was Private William Eley of the Manchester Regiment who had previously been wounded with a bullet through the ribs. 'No doubt,' said the editorial, 'he is a worthy example of the fighting stock for which the Island has always been so famous.' So, no doubt, was Private Reginald Martin, the son of the County's Horticultural Instructor, who was present at General Allenby's capture of Jerusalem from the Turks. Mrs Warren of Ventnor had by this time lost all three of her sons to the war. The last to die, Septimus, had worked on the *Isle of Wight Advertiser* before 1914.

There was a great deal of excitement – but little detail in the papers – about an aircraft that crashed in the fields near Quarr Abbey. The pilot was still alive, though badly burned and was taken to the Military Hospital at Parkhurst. Despite all this gloom and doom, the papers did their best to keep spirits up. They suggested, 'Don't moan – write cheerfully – good advice to the wives of fighting men.'

The problem for Sergeant David Jones (his unit is not given) is that he had one wife too many. Appearing before magistrates in March, he said, 'I am sorry to say the woman at Caesar's Rd [Newport] is not my lawful wife. I may as well make a clean breast of it.' He was convicted of bigamy.

More excitement happened at Seaview that month when a German mine was washed up. These things – metal globes with projecting spikes – were easily spotted in daylight but were deadly at night. The whole naval attack up the Dardanelles had been called off because of them but this one was exploded safely by the Royal Engineers.

Food hoarding outraged people and quite rightly so. The most high profile culprit nationally was the writer Marie Corelli, living in Stratford-on-Avon, although she denied it. Half a page in the *Observer* was given over to this offence on the Island involving two families, one in Ryde and one in Seaview. Generally speaking the court and the paper seem to have a surprising amount of sympathy for the accused, perhaps because, unlike Miss Corelli, the families concerned were poor. Mr E Symonds, of the Freemasons Tavern, Newport, offered five pounds 'to any charitable institution for substantial proof of the person or persons who were the instigators of the libellous report that I have been guilty of hoarding provisions contrary to the regulations issued by the Food Controller.' No one came forward.

Still on the subject of crime, the police were given a war bonus which increased their wages from £1 to 25 shillings a week. There was a great deal of interest in the appointment of the Island's first Lady Special Constable. 'Most men,' was the *Observer*'s rather arch comment, 'would consider it a privilege to be "run in" by so charming an officer.' In fact, the *Observer* was rather misleading on this. The Women Police Volunteers had first appeared on London's streets in September 1914 and the provinces followed suit. Their role was to deter women from prostitution and to carry out identity checks. No one, except arguably their founder Margaret Damer Dawson, expected them ever to do the work of policemen. They had no powers of arrest until 1922 so no-one in the Isle of Wight could have been 'run-in' by the anonymous WPC. The uniform was very unflattering – a man's tunic, peaked cap and an ankle length skirt with buttons up the side so that, in theory, a policewoman could run after miscreants.

As if to remind the world of the potential power of the United States, a poem printed in the *Morning Post* was reproduced in the *Observer*. Written by Judge Stephen C Bragaw of North Carolina, its opening lines ran –

'We are coming, Mother England, we are coming millions strong,
Hands across the sea are reaching, gripped to rid the world of
wrong...'

It was in some ways the beginning of the 'special relationship' but to most Islanders, America was far away and its usefulness probably unappreciated. 'Retreat?' US Captain Lloyd Williams said in June, 'Hell, we only just got here.' By July, 1,019,000 American troops had sailed for Europe, but they were still an 'associated power' (whatever that meant) not an Ally.

Announcements ran throughout April from Lord Rhondda, the new Food Controller (who, incidentally, was a survivor of the *Lusitania*) – 'Last year the Isle of Wight produced 3,900 tons of potatoes; consumed 7,700 tons. Plant more potatoes and make the Island self-supporting.' It was the same message churned out in the Second World War by the Ministry of Food, with the famous posters cajoling people to 'dig for victory'. There was a certain irony in both wars, however. The men who might well have planted potatoes were away fighting on various Fronts. But if people at home thought they had it bad, the prisoners at Kut had it worse. Letters were arriving from these men to their Island families describing conditions. There, butter was 15 shillings a pound; a 2lb loaf cost 2/6d and a pair of boots £10 (which would be £481 today allowing for inflation)!

War news gleaned from the National Press appears more widely from now on. General von Ludendorff's spring offensive was launched with a view to end the war before the American numbers increased, as would inevitably be the case and before the discontent at home in Germany caused a revolution. This was largely the result of the Royal Navy's blockade and near-starvation in Germany was undoubtedly a factor in reducing the will of the German people to carry on. As early as January, a cartoon in *The Bystander* by Wilmot Lunt entitled 'In Germany – Now' showed a hugely fat Food Dictator (altogether a different type from the unassuming Lord Rhondda) marching arrogantly past starving civilians. The offensive almost worked. In March, the Germans broke through the Allied lines on the Somme and by April Armentieres had fallen. By the end of May Ludendorff was only fifty miles away from Paris. Brighter news for the Allies was the death of Manfred von Richthofen, the 'Red Baron' of Jagdstaffel I, whose scarlet Fokker triplane was feared the length and breadth of the Western Front. An Australian machine-gunner brought him down on 21 April behind British lines and he was buried with full military honours.

It seems odd that despite the fact that the Allies were still generally on the back foot, there was an upbeat, holiday mood in the Island. The Island's cinemas were showing 'star films' with clear and steady pictures and seasonal bookings for the resort towns were healthy for the first time in four years. And there was a wartime romance with a happy ending. Lieutenant Charles Dawson, the poster artist, had met Lucy Dart when she sang to entertain his unit's wounded troops. He had been sketching at the time and they fell for each other. A fairytale wedding took place at Carisbrooke church. This may be a misprint in terms of the Lieutenant's Christian name. Lieutenant Montague Dawson was 23 in 1918 and served on trawlers and minesweepers. He had just been

Manfred von Richthofen

The Germans advance in the March offensive 1918.

commissioned by *The Sphere* to paint maritime subjects and after the war exhibited at the Royal Academy in London. In the 1960s he was reputedly the highest paid living artist after Picasso.

In June – before Haig's counter-offensive – Sergeant W White of the Royal Field Artillery, one of eight brothers serving somewhere in France, was awarded the Croix de Guerre for bravery. He already had the Mons Star and was mentioned twice in Despatches, having come right through from August 1914 without a scratch.

There was a huge rally in Newport to recruit more women for the Women's Land Army, another move to keep the momentum of the war effort going in the absence of men and of course, another move to female emancipation. The leaders of the Women's Suffrage Movement had made a conscious decision at the start of the war to call off their militant campaign for the duration, but by the summer of 1918 one or two letters are beginning to appear in Island papers which refer to the subject. Thousands of women had joined the Women's Volunteer Reserve or the Women's Army Auxiliary Corps after July 1917. The Women's Royal Naval Service and the Women's Royal Air Force had followed the next year, but it was an uphill struggle against the men. WAACs were given the 'rank' of officials, rather than officers; NCOs were forewomen and ORs workers. No man in any position of importance in Britain paid any attention to the shaven-headed females of the Red Army who fought in the streets of Russia along with their men. The Women's Land Army was the last attempt to galvanize females and the result – with only 16,000 volunteering – was disappointing. Cheery cartoons showed smiling farmers working alongside the girls carrying pitchforks and scythes. In practice, most male labourers were contemptuous of them, ridiculing their relative weakness.

The Voluntary Aid Detachment took women too with over 100,000 in various forces' support units by 1918. There were 6,000 WAACs in France and many more FANYs, the First Aid Nursing Yeomanry. A further 300,000 worked in munitions, creating something of a 'servant problem' for the well-to-do.

The General Post Office announced that because of 'abnormal conditions' (staff shortages) its office in Ryde would close at midday. This was a national decision – there were 12,600 post offices across the country hit in this way – but various letters make it clear that Islanders generally were not very sympathetic. In an age before telephones and radios were widely available, communication with loved ones at the Front could only be by letter; any curtailing of that would be bound to meet with disdain.

Alfred Pinhorn, a riveter from East Cowes was found guilty in the courts of illegally wearing a uniform of the Northumberland Fusiliers for four hours. The magistrate asked him why he didn't enlist and wear it legally; Pinhorn replied that he would love to, but he had a wife and children and a reserved occupation. That did not cut much ice with the Bench.

The *Daily Mail* suggested that the Island, with its subtropical climate and bracing sea air be made into one vast convalescent home for wounded soldiers. The fact was that the Island's hospitals could hardly cope as it was; to take on more would be impossible. By 8 August, when Haig's counter-offensive began near Amiens, signalling what General Ludendorff called a 'black day' for the German army, a holiday summer had returned to the Isle of Wight. Special provision had been made for the ration books of those on holiday and the bathing huts and bathing machines were in full use. Boating was still out of the question and no doubt the police and the Volunteers still kept a careful eye. There was a sense of excitement, as if, at last, the beginning of the end might be in sight.

That month the *Daily Express* carried an article, printed in the Island's papers, on the murder of the Tsar. Attributed to a 'high-ranking' Russian, it is nonsense from start to finish. Literally the only correct fact in the entire piece is the name Nicholas Romanov. There is no mention of his family at all, the implication being that he alone was shot by firing squad, having written various farewell

Consecrating the war memorial outside All Saints' Church, Ryde in 1921. The soldiers in the foreground are a guard of honour of the Isle of Wight Rifles.

letters. It has taken nearly a century for the Tsar's last moments to be known but irresponsible reporting like this was – and is? – commonplace in every newspaper in the world. Then no one doubted the headlines or knew about Lord Rothermere's admission of lies – the National Press said that the Germans were everywhere on the run and the war would soon be over.

There was talk of a war memorial to commemorate the dead of the Great War, 'not for the present generation but for those who came after'. At first (in July) this was to be set up in Winchester, in effect incorporating the Island's Hampshire contingent in the larger regiment. When there was an outcry over this, the idea was to erect a single memorial in Newport, as the Island's county town. That, too, was deemed unacceptable and individual parishes decided to erect their own. All Saints and St John's wanted one each in Ryde; so did virtually every church in the Island.

In October, by which time the Allies had smashed through the German Hindenburg line with their tanks, the great and good of Ryde were arguing whether the war memorial should be set up along the Strand, near an older memorial to the dead of the *Royal George* which capsized with huge loss of life at Spithead in August 1782.

The Gothic war memorial inside All Saints' Church Ryde. *(Trow)*

The war memorial in St Thomas's Square, Newport, typical of the granite obelisks erected all over the Wight in the 1920s. *(Trow)*

Ryde cinema showed DW Griffiths' epic *Birth of a Nation* in September – 'one of the finest pictures that has ever been screened'. It was shown in twelve parts, running for three and a half hours and booking to see it was essential.

Freshwater war memorial in November 2013, in the churchyard of St John's. The individual crosses have been placed there by families remembering their own dead. *(Trow)*

The war memorial in Yarmouth. This one is quite unusual in having a crucifix on top of it.
(Trow)

Personal War Notes now fill a whole page in Island newspapers, reflecting the confidence of journalists who had the leisure and the momentum to write more than they had done for much of the war. Stories of German brutality meted out to British prisoners dominated the headlines and, merely a footnote at this stage, influenza had broken out in various parts of Europe and even, as early as May, in Cowes. This was the 'plague of the Spanish lady' (actually a strain of the flu virus from America) which would wipe out 250,000 Britons by the end of 1919. The cartoonist William Heath Robinson, the 'gadget king' of his day, had predicted such an outbreak as early as June 1915.

For the first time in October, the *Observer* carried a pictorial supplement with photographs from the Front and munitions factories (none of them particularly relevant to Islanders) and 'Kitchen Recipes in War Time'. Potato and carrot soup was one idea; so was creamed fish and haricots, savoury lentils and savoury ox heart. Why not follow this with chocolate pudding?

On 31 August, the editor of the *County Press* wrote –

'We have to make the German people, the swashbucklers of Europe and the enemies of civilisation, realise, and the whole world realise, that they are beaten. A peace by negotiation for us at least would mean industrial ruin, economic vassalage and national disaster.'

In October, the demand was the same – 'their blood [the dead of the Isle of Wight] calls for complete victory and unconditional surrender'. There was a deep irony here. By suing for an armistice as early as 3 October, General von Ludendorff prevented the invasion of Germany itself and kept the armed forces' reputation intact. Out of this, from the German army's point of view, arose the notion of 'stab in the back', espoused by the Nazi party and indeed most Germans, that the Kaiser's government had sold out to the Allies and that this was a political betrayal. And, as things turned out, everything that the *County Press* editorial of August warned against, happened anyway, no matter what sort of surrender took place. The huge cost of the war, in terms of manpower and materiel, *did* cause 'industrial ruin, economic vassalage and national disaster'. The General Strike of 1926, the Wall Street Crash of 1929, the coalition government of 1931, the Jarrow March of 1936 – arguably none of this would have happened were it not for the Great War. All we could be sure of was that conditions would be *far* worse in defeated Germany.

The end of the war was reported by Island papers in a low key way. Turkey had surrendered on 30 October and the Union Jack and the Italian Tricolore flew side by side over Ryde's town hall to celebrate Austria-Hungary's surrender on 3 November, but the Military Tribunals continued, trenchant as ever and, with only two days fighting to go, the list of dead and wounded fills two thirds of a page of the *Observer*. The *County Press* wrote, 'An armistice signed at 5am on Monday November 11th brought to an end the greatest war in history. Six hours later hostilities ceased on all Fronts, on the 11th hour of the 11th day of the 11th month of the year.'

That same day the last of the Tribunals was heard for East Wight at Ryde Town Hall and all fifteen cases of exemption were granted. The Isle of Wight

County Hospital passed a resolution five days later, that the Committee 'desire to place on record their humble and heartfelt gratitude to Almighty God, for the victory He has been pleased to grant to our cause.'

The Ministry of Labour announced that recruiting and call-up notices were cancelled and the celebrations began. In Newport the Mayor, Alderman FE Whitcher, read out a notice that all business in the town should be suspended from 11.30am until 2.00pm so that everyone could meet outside the Town Hall. It was literally feet from here that the first casualty of the war had died, as a result of a gas explosion, four years and one month earlier. The news of the Armistice had come through from Parkhurst Barracks and official confirmation had been posted in the *County Press* window. Sergeant Osborne ran up the Union Jack and the Red Ensign over the Guildhall to rapturous cheers from the huge

The town hall at Ryde has its own war memorial, with five panels listing the names of the dead. The poppy wreaths are a permanent reminder of Flanders Fields. *(Trow)*

A wreath laid by the Royal Hampshire Regiment in November 2013. The Isle of Wight Rifles formed the 2/8th Battalion of the regiment during the Great War. *(Trow)*

crowd. Flags and ribbons of red, white and blue appeared from nowhere and filled the centre of the town. The church bells rang and services of thanksgiving followed the speeches. The euphoria was of course tinged with sadness – 'here and there in the happy throng,' a reporter noted, 'there were sad faces and moist eyes for dear ones who will never return ...'

In Ryde soon after ten o'clock, a notice appeared in the *County Press* window in Union Street. The bells of the town's churches rang out at eleven and the main streets were crowded with people. A huge crowd outside the Town Hall cheered and sang 'patriotic airs'. That night the place was lit up by fireworks which were 'let off promiscuously, the juvenile portion of the community taking a prominent part to their hearts' delight in this direction...' For once, no one minded and if the 'flog 'em school' itched to reach for their birches, we did not hear about it.

In Cowes, the heart of the Island's munitions industry which had done its best for four long years, there were flags everywhere, like Cowes Week in the now distant days before the war. In the shipyards, all the workers downed tools and joined the revellers in the streets, which rang with their songs. Apart from aircraft, they had built twenty-two destroyers, eleven patrol boats and three submarines. Here and there in the crowd were the khaki uniforms of the men who had given their all and the sirens of the factories and those of ships out to sea added to the cacophony and the hysteria of the day.

Cease-fires might be ordered; armistices arranged. The guns, great and small, might fall silent. And it is in that silence that the toll is counted and the fears grow. There is no accurate number of the men of the Wight who fell in the Great War; it is likely to be nearly 2000. Some of these had no graves because their bodies were never found.

Not all of them ended up with their names chiselled into memorials on the Island or in the theatres of war throughout the world. Sadly, 'their names' do not 'liveth for ever more'. One of the last men back from the Front was the ex-policeman Owen Palmer of the BEF, who had been in the thick of things from the beginning. He had won the Military Medal and a wound stripe.

'It will not be long,' hoped the *Observer*, 'before we enjoy the same liberties as we did prior to the war ... DORA is dying a natural death and there will not be much grief at her funeral.' The Defence of the Realm Consolidated Act had been in existence since 27 November 1914 and two more Acts had become law five months later. The army and navy had been given virtually absolute powers over all buildings and property in their area. The authorities had directed labour, opened and closed workplaces. They had banned public meetings and sporting fixtures. They had interned Aliens, controlled the movement of a free people. They had censored the Press and letters from the Front. They had set up Tribunals to catch draft-dodgers and controlled the amount of food that went into people's mouths. Most of these extraordinarily arbitrary regulations were dropped in the weeks after the Armistice, but those relating to public houses and intoxicating liquors stayed. And if the Home Front of 1914-18 thought they had it rough, all they had to do was survive until 1939 to see it all happening all over again with a vengeance.

In London, the warhorses that had survived (and vast numbers had not) were auctioned off, with the names of the men who rode them written on their bridles so that they had first refusal. It is not known whether any Islanders took advantage of this. Such was the sentimentality that Fortunino Matania's painting for *The Sphere* in June 1916 became the most popular propaganda piece of the entire war. Entitled 'Goodbye, Old Man' it shows a Gunner of the Royal Field Artillery cradling the head of his horse on a shell-strewn road somewhere in France.

According to the War Graves Commision the last man in the British Army to be killed in the Great War was Private Edward Sullivan of A Company, 7th Corps, the Cyclist Battalion, from East Ham in London. He too had come all through the war since August 1914 and he died just minutes before eleven o'clock.

'They think it's all over.' And it was. The children of Barton School, Newport, which lost many old boys during the war, taking part in peace celebrations, 1919.

For some it was 'business as usual' as the Island's papers trumpeted – '**Good News!** The Vectis Rupture Brace will give you comfort. **Peace** and contentment if you eat wholesome foods'. The indefatigable World's Stores in Ryde was already looking forward to the homecoming Christmas – 'Do justice to your Victory Christmas.' And two soldiers appeared before the courts charged with drunk and disorderly behaviour. 'Tommy Atkins' was still being a nuisance. The war poet Edward Shanks, invalided out in 1915, summed it up brilliantly –

'And some will misremember what once they learnt with pain
And hit a bloody sergeant and go to clink again.'

It was a brave new world. The Special Constables held a special supper before disbandment and Thanksgiving Peace dances were held wherever there was a suitable hall to hold the celebrants. Two captured U-boats sailed the Solent into Portsmouth Harbour and the public were urged to inspect them at minimal cost, the proceeds of which would go to the spectacular war memorial on the Front at Southsea.

'Have the Germans won?' a banner headline in the National Press asked and the doubts had set in from the first day of Peace. 700,000 British soldiers, airmen and sailors had died, as had 14,600 Merchant Seamen. 1,117 civilians had been killed in bombing raids and coastal bombardments. Including the Canadians, who lost 60,000 of their 620,000 men committed and the Australians who lost 18,000 casualties from 330,000 sent in and the New Zealanders who lost over half of their contingent and the Indians who lost 60,000, the Empire lost almost a million men – the lost generation who were an incalculable loss in the years ahead. Many people ignored this reality. Throughout the 1920s everyone got used to men hobbling on crutches, men with one arm, men with artificial faces. No-one ever quite got used to the nightmares, the tears, the rasping voices of gas survivors and the fear of loud noises. A more sympathetic generation would come to terms with all this in the years ahead, before the guts and heroism of the Great War were eclipsed by another one twenty-one years later. For now, in the Isle of Wight, in the late autumn of 1918, there was a brief economic boom; the place was a home fit for heroes and the 'war to end wars' was over.

Index